a guide to the
PICTISH
STONES

a guide to the
PICTISH
STONES

Elizabeth Sutherland
Photographs by Tom E. Gray

Birlinn

Dedication

For Ania who discovered so many of these stones with me

First published in Great Britain, 1997 by
Birlinn Limited
14 High Street
Edinburgh EH1 1TE

Text © Elizabeth Sutherland, 1997
Photographs © Tom E. Gray, 1997

ISBN 1-874744-66-1

British Library Cataloguing-in-Publication Data
A Catalogue record of this book is available
from the British Library

Designed and typeset in 9/11pt Leawood
by Janet Watson

Printed and bound in Finland by
Werner Söderström OY

CONTENTS

Acknowledgements

I would like to thank the following museums, individuals and organisations for their help in compiling this Guide.

Historic Scotland for their leaflets and guides to Meigle, St. Vigean's and St. Andrew's Museums.

Royal Commission on the Ancient & Historical Monuments of Scotland for their *List of Pictish Symbol Stones* 1994.

National Museums of Scotland for their handlist of stones on display or in store 1981.

Inverness Museum and Art Gallery for their *Catalogue of Class I Pictish Stones* 1949.

The Pictish Art Society for their invaluable information contained in their Newsletters and Journals.

The **Society of Antiquaries of Scotland** for their Proceedings and Papers.

The **Council for Scottish Archaeology** for their annual journal, *Discovery and Exploration in Scotland.*

The editor and contributors to **Scottish Archaeological News.**

The many curators of local museums who have sent me catalogues and information in Lerwick, Orkney, Thurso, Dunrobin Castle, Groam House Museum and Ross and Cromarty Museums' Service, Tarbat Trust, Inverness, Elgin, Inverurie, Anthropological Museum Marischal College, University of Aberdeen, Montrose, Perth, Meffan Institute Forfar and Angus Museums' Service, Dundee, Historic Scotland for Meigle and St. Vigeans Museums.

The Editor of the Pinkfoot Press for reprinting *The Early Christian Monuments of Scotland* by J. Romilly Allen and Joseph Anderson thus making so much information immediately accessible.

The following individuals all of whom have helped me in different ways: Norman Atkinson, Ian Fisher, Jill Harden, Isabel Henderson, Anthony Jackson, Marianna Lines, Edwina Proudfoot, Anna Ritchie, Niall M. Robertson, Ian Shepherd, Michael Spearman, Val Turner, Graham Watson, Ann Watters and many others who have shared with me their knowledge of individual stones and sites.

Above all, I want to thank Tom E. Gray not only for providing his superb photographs but also for his invaluable information throughout.

Elizabeth Sutherland

INTRODUCTION

Who were the Picts? What do their symbols mean? Where are the carved stones? These are the questions most people ask and there are many books and academic papers that try to explain their history, art and archaeology. But because the Picts were a Dark Age nation there are few answers that don't require to be qualified by the words – possibly, probably and perhaps.

This Guide sets out to reply to the only question that can be answered with some accuracy – the position of the carved stones today. Over the years many have been moved from their original sites and placed in museums for safe-keeping with a number of stones, fragments and casts stored or displayed in the National Museums of Scotland at Edinburgh. Others are inside or outside local churches, museums, in private grounds and stately homes, or standing in the open landscape. They are still being found by the plough, in excavations or by a pair of sharp eyes, at the rate of one or two a year. 1995 was an exceptional year with some twenty important finds.

On your journey of discovery remember that these relics are fragile and should not be touched, chalked, rubbed or polluted in any way. Amazingly, many have survived for some 1500 years in spite of weathering, deliberate destruction, neglect and mutilation by some of our ancestors. A leaflet available from Historic Scotland tells us how best to care for them today.

To appreciate them properly first you have to see them. All that I can find are included in this Guide, even those which have been recorded in the past but now are lost. If so many have survived, how many more must there have once been? How many more are yet to be found? An exciting thought.

Who were the Picts?

The Pictish nation emerged from a collection of warrior Celtic tribes who, centuries BC, had emigrated from Europe into Northern Britain. They first came into documented history as a nation in AD 297 when a Roman writer, Eumenius, wrote that the Britons were accustomed only to fighting 'their half-naked enemies – the Picts and the Irish'. Thus they became a historical people at that point with a collective name and they remained a united nation until about AD 840 when the Irish Scot, Kenneth Mac Alpin defeated them, and the land of the Picts became known as Scotland.

They probably got their name 'Painted Ones' from the Roman soldiers who patrolled the Antonine wall and had to deal with them face-to-face. The Irish called them Cruithni which translates as 'people of the designs'. It is almost certain that they tattooed or painted their faces and bodies. What they called themselves is not known.

Where were the Picts?

The borders between the Picts, Britons and Angles south of the Clyde/Forth valley and, after AD 500, the Scots from Ireland who settled in Argyll, were fairly fluid. But the heart of Pictland was centred in Tayside, Grampian and Highland regions, the territory north and north-east of the Antonine wall including Orkney and Shetland but excluding Strathclyde. Before AD 500, they ruled as far as the Outer Hebrides. As late as c.565 the Scottish saint Columba thought it appropriate to ask permission from the Pictish King Brude in Inverness to establish his Scottish monastery in Iona. Isolated symbol stones can still be seen in Skye, Wester Ross and Argyll, but the majority are to be found east of Drumalban, that great spiny watershed formed by mountains that extend the length of Scotland nearer the west coast.

Pictish place names

There are many surviving Pictish place names, of which the most important is *Pit,* meaning a portion of land. Thus when we visit Pitlochry, Pittenweem, Pitodrie or Pitcaple – about 100 place names in all include *Pit* – we know that the Picts were there before us.

Pictish society

The Picts lived in a pyramidal society ruled by a high king, provincial kings and a warrior/priesthood elite. Craftsmen such as ironsmiths, jewellers, bronze-workers and sculptors were well-respected and had their workshops close to or inside the royal forts or palaces. On a par with craftsmen were probably horse-breeders and land-owning farmers. Pictish economy was based on agriculture.

Apart from the elite, the Picts were principally cowboys whose farming methods were to change little over the centuries until the disastrous Battle of Culloden (1746).

The King List

A list of high kings, their names, dates and the names of their fathers has survived in several forms as the only piece of near-contemporary documentary evidence thought to have come from the Picts themselves. It was probably kept in Iona or one of the Pictish monasteries – we don't know which – and fortunately copied by Irish annalists. This record is considered accurate from c.550 and the reign of Brude mac Maelcon in Inverness.

Pictish succession

What the list does not explain is why none of the kings inherited high kingship from their natural fathers at least until the end of the Pictish era and the creation of the great new dynasty founded by Kenneth Mac Alpin, King of the Scots.

This has led some scholars to believe in the foundation legend probably invented by Irish druids to account for the existence of the Picts as follows. An army of Pictish mercenaries arrived in Ireland from Scythia to assist the Irish king in defeating his enemies, which they duly did. In order to get rid of these powerful warriors, the Irish king told them there was territory in northern Britain ripe for the taking and gave them Irish princesses to start their own dynasty on condition that kingly inheritance went through these Irish wives – in other words, matrilinear succession.

Possible Pictish matriliny

Many scholars, the Venerable Bede from Northumberland included, believed this slice of Irish propaganda, which would be one way of accounting for the fact that no high king inherited kingship from his natural father, though in several instances he inherited from his brother(s). In short, when a king died, it was not his son who inherited but his sister's son. We don't know the Picts' own foundation legend, but it would probably have been very different.

Other scholars see the succession as a matter of electing

the fittest man for the job out of several dynasties throughout Pictland, a thoroughly Celtic way of ensuring that high kingship went to the ablest man. There are many arguments for and against the possibility of matriliny among the Picts. We simply don't know the answer. What is more certain is that no queen – as far as we know – ruled in her own right.

Pictish settlements
Most Pictish settlements apart from those in Orkney and Shetland have not survived because the buildings were made of wood. Homesteads were mainly round timber houses set in enclosures to keep wild beasts out and domestic animals safe. Close to many of these dwellings were souterrains or crescent-shaped, stone-lined underground dwellings which may have been used for religious reasons but more probably for storage. Aerial photography of crop-marks is beginning to disclose increasingly more sites, including large timber halls which may have been royal palaces or places of assembly and feasting. Duns, hill-forts, vitrified forts and crannogs were also inhabited, though many of these date from the Iron Age. Duns and crannogs survived as dwellings long after the Pictish era whereas brochs by this time were well out-of-date.

Pictish language
Until the coming of Christianity and Latin, the Picts had no written language. In other parts of the Celtic world we know that the druids discouraged reading and writing because their whole system of communication was based on memory. Picts spoke a form of Gaelic which was not the same as Irish Gaelic, more akin to Welsh, lost to us today. However in the 4th century an Irishman invented the Ogam script, which you will see on several Pictish stones. This alphabet, consisting of letters called after trees and shrubs, was based on the Latin alphabet and looked like little twigs on or across a central stem. Ogam communication was used almost exclusively for inscriptions.

Pictish art and music
The Picts are credited with inventing the triangular harp which appears on some six stones. Drums, horns and triple pipes are also illustrated on the stones.

As metal-workers in bronze, silver and gold their work is unsurpassed, as is evident from the various treasure troves unearthed from St Ninian's Isle in Shetland to Norrie's Law in Fife.

But it is sculpture that makes this typical Dark Age warrior nation unique. The carved stones are a sumptuous inheritance, a blend of art and craft that repay our interest and fire our admiration. Enjoy your journey.

STONES AND SYMBOLS

Three classes of sculpture

The stones fall into three groups as defined in *The Early Christian Monuments of Scotland* by J. Romilly Allen and Joseph Anderson (hereafter known as ECMS).

Class I (hereafter C.I) consists of groups or pairs of symbols simply incised on undressed boulders or Neolithic and Bronze Age monoliths. There is a theory – but only a theory – that these symbols were first tattooed on skin, tooled in leather and carved on wood, before being incised on stone in probably the 6th century. Thus the symbols may have been much older than their stone versions. C.I. stones continued to be carved well into the Christian period. Some include Ogam inscriptions.

Possible reasons for raising C.I stones:

(a) To communicate important marriages in a matrilinear system

(b) To proclaim territorial boundaries or ownership by the use of heraldic totems

(c) To mark places of magical significance to the local settlement

(d) To indicate burial grounds or act as tombstones for the elite

(e) To form distance markers

(f) Combinations of above.

Class II (hereafter C.II) are usually cross-slabs, though they may also be parts of box shrines, altar screens or recumbent monuments. They consist of dressed slabs of local stone carved in relief with the cross and decoration on the front and ornate C.I symbols with interlace, figure and animal images and sometimes a second cross on the back. These date from the establishment of an official Pictish Church in the early 8th century until the end of the Pictish era.

Possible reasons for erection of C.II stones:

(a) Raised to the glory of God and in memory of the person represented by the symbols

(b) Raised by the person represented by the symbols to the glory of God in memory of an important battle, event or person

(c) Variations or combinations of the above.

The cross-slab, like medieval stained-glass windows, was meant to educate the illiterate, to be preached on and taught from by the ecclesiastics.

Class III stones (hereafter known as C.III) are the same as C.II but show no Pictish symbols.

Early Christian (hereafter EC) are boulders or dressed slabs lightly or more heavily carved with a cross. These are hard to date for they could come at any time in the EC period. Some are grave-markers from old kirkyards and others would seem to mark shrines or prayer stations for pilgrims. Not all are mentioned in the text.

Symbols

A symbol is a creature, object or abstract design that usually, but not always, occurs more than once on the stones – a shorthand means of communication for a race that had no written language. The interpretation is based almost entirely on guess-work. Most, but not all, C.I symbols also appear on C.II stones. A few C.II symbols do not appear on C.I stones. They fall into six groups with approximate number of appearances in both classes as follows:

1. The rods

V-rod. Nearly always connected to the crescent. Possibly stands for crossed sceptres, divining rod, lightning rod or broken arrow, perhaps indicating death of a symbol-owner or protection by dead warrior ancestors.

Z-rod. Crosses several symbols. Possibly signifies a broken spear indicating death of symbol owner, or ancestral warrior protection.

2. Realistic celtic cult creatures

Snake. 14 appearances on C.I stones: 5 on C.II. Wisdom and healing, renewal and immortality. (Also with Z-rod).

Salmon 14:6. Knowledge and second sight. Seen as magic because it could pass safely between salt water, fresh water and air.

Eagle 11:4. Chieftainship, justice and truth. St John.

Bull 9:1 Strength, potency and fertility.

Boar 4:0 Power. Nourishment to dead and living.

Wolf 3:0 Cunning, predatory, rapacious.

Goose 4:0. Vigilance. Ferocity. Protection.

Stag 1:0. Forest God evoked by hunters for success. Fertility, power, kingship.

Horse 1:0. Worship of horse goddess Epona. Power, vitality, majesty, magic, prophecy. Transporter to the Otherworld.

?Seal 2:0. Enchantment. Shape-shifting.

Man 4:0. Some see the man as
a symbol representing
e.g. kingship and power.

3. Fantastic beasts

Pictish beast *c.* 29:22. Kelpie or water-horse – power over
water. ?Dolphin.

Beast-heads 4:4 Several versions representing possibly
dog or deer, horse or seal. Cult of head as seat of spirit.

4. Object symbols

Mirror and comb 49:9 (not always together). Elite women.

Arch (?horse-shoe) 13:1. Rainbow bridge between this and
the Otherworld. Immortality. Also with V-rod, 0:1.

Cauldron 7:5. Celtic regeneration. Plenty. Healing. Associated with Dagda the Good.

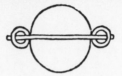

Broken sword, tuning fork or tongs 8:2. Death of warrior. Musicianship and ironsmith when associated with anvil.

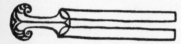

?Anvil 2:1. Associated with ironsmith.

Hammer 1:1. Associated with ironsmith.

Bow and arrow or Helmet 1:0. Impossible to describe more clearly. Probably neither.

5. Geometric symbols

Crescent & V-rod 62:23. Probably associated with moon. Royalty, fertility, regeneration and the tides.

Crescent without V-rod 17:3.

Double crescent 3:1.

Double-disc & Z-rod 32:25. Often associated with the Druidic duality of the sun which lights this world by day and the Otherworld by night. The sun's two faces, benign in summer, malevolent in winter.

Double-disc without rod 14:10.

Disc & rectangle
(also known as mirror-case)
13:4. Burial cairn,
wheel house, solar wheel.

Disc & notched rectangle
3:0. Solar wheel held up
by human figure?

Three discs in circle 6:1. Celtic triple-headed goddess.
Circular brooch symbolising status. Horse ornament or
three pots in a kiln.

Rectangle 19:3. Container for tools. Kist representing possessions and spoils of war. Satchel for travel and on C.IIs for carrying Gospel books.

Notched rectangle & Z-rod 12:2. Chariot and horses.
Fortress. Possibly a warrior's symbol.

Notched rectangle without Z-rod 1:0. in E. Wemyss cave.

Stepped rectangle 1:3. ?Anvil or forge.

L-Shaped rectangle 1:2.

Triple oval 4:1. May represent arm bracelet.

6. *Abstract symbols*

Flower 5:4. Plant or possibly piece of horse decoration e.g. bronze harness brooch.

S-shaped figure 4:0. Possible horse decoration.

Square with corner scroll 1:0. Found on Kintore 4 in 1974. Impossible to decipher. Perhaps applied bronze plate.

Triquetra 0:4. Odin's knot or, in Christian terms, the Unity of the Trinity.

Meigle 8 Symbol 0:1. May be a symbol, but appears only once so far.

Class II symbols which occur more than once on the stones include most of the C.I with the addition of the following:

1. People

Women: 6 or 7. Perhaps representing the Virgin Mary or other Biblical women.

Warriors: Elite of Pictish society. Battle scenes.

Hunters: (a) with hounds and wounded hind – Divine Hunt where hounds and forces of evil attack human soul.

Hunters: (b) elite in heaven, the 'happy hunting ground'.

Human head held between two monsters: Human soul held up by power symbols.

Monks: Church and possibly founding saints.

Bird- and animal-masked men: Evil spirits or devils. Delilah on Inchbrayock 1 is shown with a beast-head.

Old and New Testament figures: Adam and Eve, King David, Samson, Daniel, Jonah, Virgin and Child, Peter and Paul, the two hermits, Paul and Anthony, Raising of Lazarus, the Transfiguration, and the 12 Apostles or 12 Tribes of Israel, etc. These represent prefigurations, deeds and miracles of Christ.

King David: 6 or 7. Usually with harp, sheep and lion. Kingship.

Four Evangelists: Lion of St Mark, Eagle of St John, Calf of St Luke, and Man of St Matthew.

2. Classical and Christian creatures

Centaur: gave healing plant to Greek God of medicine so may represent Christ the Healer.

Sagittarius: another centaur.

Icthus (fish): Christ.

Angels, devils, imps.

Creatures: hounds, monkeys, birds, deer, boar, snakes, seahorses, hippocampi.

3. Fantastic beasts

Lion-like creatures with tails between legs or along back may represent St Mark, but may equally come from a Bestiary. The Bestiary lion when hunted obliterates its footprints with its tail so that the hunters cannot follow; so Christ, unseen governs the world.

Hind-like beasts with legs doubled up beneath their bodies may represent the human soul beset by danger on its journey to salvation.

Other Bestiary creatures might be griffins, manticoras, dragons and an assortment of reptiles each with its own Christian interpretation, most of which is not known today.

4. Other symbols

Plants: foliage, trees, vines and grapes, might symbolise the Tree of Life or salvation within the Church through the Eucharist.

Objects: harps, triple pipes, hunting horns, dirks, daggers and axes, swords and spears, round, square and rectangular shields, staffs or croziers, flabella (liturgical fans).

Brooches seen on Wester Denoon and possibly Hilton of Cadboll and other figures may denote important women or badges of office.

Crosses: ECMS describes 49 different shapes and sizes of cross, each individually decorated and designed, so that no two are the same. They represent Christ in Glory. Cross slabs or outline crosses with the figure of Christ on them such as Camus (p.118) represent the Crucifixion.

Decorations: an extraordinary variety of intricate interlace in knotwork, spirals, key pattern and many-corded plait-work, bosses and snake bosses. Bearing in mind that every design, scene and object on all these stones is layered with symbolism, it is impossible today to discover the totality of meaning that lies hidden within the wealth of designs.

NOTES, ABBREVIATIONS AND SYMBOLS

Each stone is individually described (as far as possible) as follows:

    Class I, II, III or EC (Early Christian)

    Type of stone (e.g. ORS for Old Red Sandstone)

    Approximate height of stone

    Brief descripion of the original site, finding, and condition

    Ordnance Survey Number and/or name of present position

    Description of stone and symbols

    Comment if necessary

Each stone is numbered and arranged alphabetically in the text to correspond to its number on the maps (* showing former locations), where relevant.

The more important Pictish Centres are numbered **1M**. Some Pictish sites without stones come at the end of each chapter. They are marked alphabetically.

Abbreviations and symbols

✤	Stone in museum
✤	Stone lost or in private hands. *Always* ask permission of owners to visit private sites.
C.I II III	Categories or classes of stones
EC	Early Christian
ECMS	Early Christian Monuments of Scotland
NTS	National Trust of Scotland
ORS	Old Red Sandstone
PS	Pictish symbol(s)
NMS	National Museums of Scotland

THE PICTISH KINGDOMS

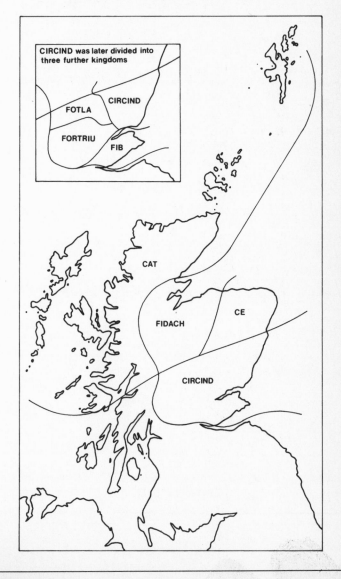

CIRCIND was later divided into three further kingdoms

FOTLA

CIRCIND

FORTRIU

FIB

CAT

FIDACH

CE

CIRCIND

EDINBURGH AND SOUTH OF THE FORTH

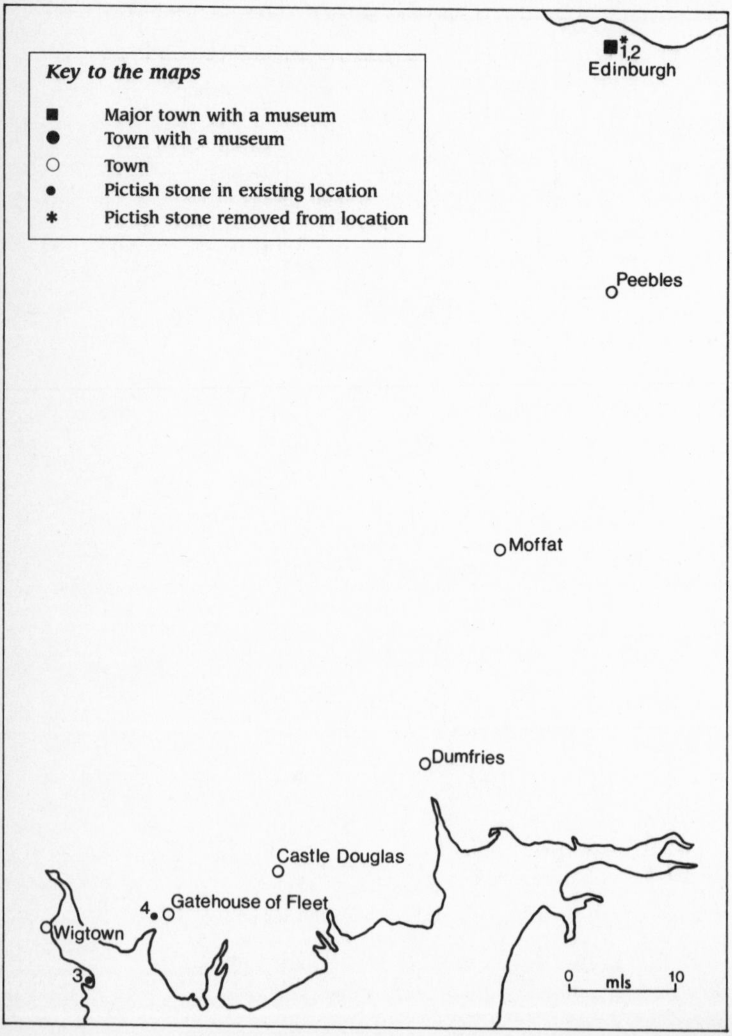

■✳1,2
Edinburgh

○ Peebles

○ Moffat

○ Dumfries

Castle Douglas
○

4 •○ Gatehouse of Fleet

○ Wigtown

3 •

0   mls   10

National Museums of Scotland

1 Your pilgrimage to discover one of the earliest and greatest treasures of our nation – the Pictish Sculptured Stones – must include a visit to the **National Museums of Scotland** in Queen Street and Chamber Street, Edinburgh **(NMS)**. Here are some 150 carved stones from all over the country, gathered together for protection and conservation against further weathering and human vandalism. There are also many casts of stones, which make a valuable record for those future generations who are bound to find the stones still in the open to be further decayed by weathering and pollution.

Cast-making is a craft that is continually improving so that you can often see the patterns and figures more clearly than on the originals. Dunfallandy from Pitlochry, now in Groam House Museum, Dupplin near Perth, and the Aberlemno Churchyard stone, now in the Meffan Centre, Forfar, are prime examples of what good casting can reproduce.

At the moment the majority of NMS stones are in store but it is to be hoped that when the new Dark Age section is completed many more will be on display or at least placed in a position more easily accessible to visitors.

Computer enhancement, still in early stages, may be a better way of recording the stones for posterity. Then perhaps it will be possible for the mother museum to return to her offspring country-wide the stones that once stood in their vicinity.

Meanwhile, no student of Pictish art, and no newcomer to the Pictish world should miss the display in Edinburgh when it re-opens in 1998.

2 Edinburgh ✠ **C.I.** Sandstone. 3 ft 8 in (112 cm) tall. This was found in use as a footbridge in Princes Street Gardens immediately below the castle. **NMS** IB 1.
PS: a crescent & V-rod above part of a double disc and Z-rod.

South of the River Forth

Among the sculptured stones which owe their presence to Northumbrian influence there are a few Pictish symbol stones south of the Forth which should be mentioned. Although never strictly part of Pictland, Pictish travellers and raiders, according to literary evidence, must have known it very well. There is one Pit place-name in East Lothian at Pitcox.

3 Eggerness displays a series of carvings on a rock-face and nearby outcrop discovered in 1986. The stones are kept under a layer of turf the better to protect them. North of Garlieston in Wigtownshire NX 48 47.

PS: a fine stag on the rock-face and, on the outcrop, several ponies with their heads turned back over their shoulders. Also a hoof-print complete with the 'frog' in the sole. Bearing in mind the prints found in Dunino Den and Dunadd fortress, could this site be connected to coronations?

4 Trusty's Hill was the site of a hill-fort near Anwoth at NX 588 560. A rocky outcrop which flanks the entrance bears a number of **C.I** symbols. The name Trusty seems to be a derivation of Drust or Drostan which is a Pictish name.

PS: on the left a double-disc & z-rod; at the top, a small human face with two horns ending in spirals protruding from the head. On the right, a seahorse with spiralled tail and, pointing at its belly, what looks like a dagger with a semi-circular spiralled terminal.

Fife, Kinross
and Stirlingshire

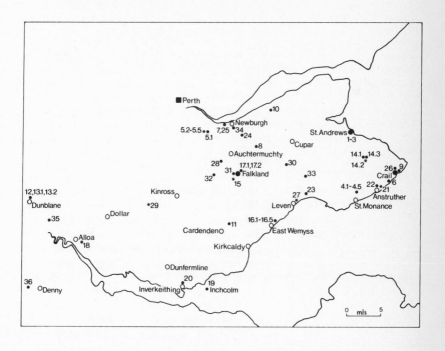

St Andrews

St Andrews, in the Dark Ages, was known as Kilrimont (Church of the King's Mount). Unfortunately its early history has been complicated by later medieval attempts to try to prove that the Scottish Church was older and superior to the English foundation.

According to one legend the Pictish King Angus I mac Fergus is though to have established the cult of St Andrew in the 8th century. Legend relates that St Rule or Regulus, a Greek monk, brought sacred relics (a tooth, knee-cap, arm-bone and three fingers) of the apostle from Constantinople and paraded them with king and court round the consecrated ground in St Andrews, where they erected twelve stone crosses in his honour.

Another interpretation associates Angus II (also mac Fergus) with St Rule in founding St Andrews a century later. We don't know for certain.

1 **St Andrews Cathedral Museum** ✢ contains a great wealth of sculptured stones. More than 50 fragments alone were found when excavating the foundations of **St Mary of the Rock** north of the Cathedral overlooking the harbour. Some fragments were found in the town and many others in the Cathedral walls and surrounds. Their style is evidence of the strong connection between Picto/ Celtic art and the Northumbrian style between the 8th and 10th centuries AD. There is no space in this guide to name them all. Go and see them for yourselves.

2 **St Andrews Sarcophagus** ✢ is undoubtedly one of the finest pieces of early medieval European art and demonstrates perfectly the blending of Pictish and Anglian art forms. This magnificent shrine dating from the late 8th or early 9th centuries was probably commissioned to hold sacred relics – perhaps those of St Andrew himself – and designed to be housed inside the ancient monastery that preceded the Cathedral. Found in 1833 while grave-digging near St Rule's Tower buried over 6 ft (183 cm) deep.

Front: shows in finest detail three aspects of King David the hunter and shepherd. From right to left, find a large David with curled hair, elaborate clothing and decorated dagger. As shepherd, he is rending the jaws of a curly-maned lion. Over his shoulders find an admiring woolly sheep and an impish monkey. In the upper centre, David as hunter is mounted with a hawk

on arm, face-to-face with a leaping beast of prey.
Below, David in plaid with hunting dog and spear stalks
a variety of animals. Behind him a griffin has settled
its claws in a mule's back and bites its neck. Far left,
the ?Tree of Life shelters some strange creatures.

The symbolism contained in this scene is no doubt as
rich and multi-layered as the exquisite and detailed carving itself. David is seen as a prefiguration of Christ and
symbolic of kingship.

3 St Andrews

3.9: ✤ C.III. *c.* 2 ft (61 cm) high. Cross-slab tapering upwards.
Front: a single panel with key-pattern design which
could be seen as a cross above two figures facing left.
A smaller man holds book within an enclosure held
with both hands by a larger bearded figure. (?Raising
of Lazarus).

3.19: ✤ C.III. *c.* 8 ft (244 cm) tall. Cross-shaft originally
built (with others) into the basal course of the east end of
the cathedral (*c.* AD 1160) and removed for display in
1909. These stones would probably have stood outside
within monastic grounds.
Front: divided into three panels: (1) Two bearded
figures, one holding sword, the other a shield, face
each other over the head of a smaller figure. Dr
Henderson suggests this may be ritual initiation of
youth into warrior, or in Christian terms, 'putting on
the armour of righteousness'. Above, scroll foliage
may represent the Tree of Life. (2) Two birds sit on
the head and shoulders of a man facing forwards.
He seems to be attached to two animal bodies.
(3) Key pattern.

3.24: ✤ C.III. Top of a cross-slab found in the cathedral
wall. This 'rule and compass' design consists of one
panel showing double-beaded cross with angular armpits
and ring filled with crisp key-pattern. Two rectangles of
key-pattern lie either side of top arm above ring.

3.28 and 3.29: ✤ Fragments that together show ?David
as harpist. Dr Anna Ritchie suggests they may be part of
missing back panel of Sarcophagus or of another shrine.

4 Abercrombie

Five C.III fragments of cross-slabs are built
into the church walls. NO 523 034.

4.l: unadorned cross. The background panels are filled with 4-cord plait-work.
Left side: single panel of spirals.

4.la: seems to be the lower portion of 4.l. The background to the shaft and left edge show the same spiral work.

4.2: Sandstone. 3½ ft (107 cm) tall. The background shows four panels of assorted interlace and key-patterns.

4.3: Sandstone. 4¼ ft (130 cm) tall. Carved on one side only.
Front: ornamented with small recessed squares in the arms and centre of the cross which stands on a curved base.

4.4: Sandstone *c.* 2 ft (61 cm) high. Fragment showing part of a vertical panel containing a lion, boar and man.

4.5: small fragment of sandstone with double spiral and pattern of straight lines.

5 Abernethy in the 8th century was an important royal ecclesiastic centre. The round tower is all that remains of the monastery that may have been built here between the 9th and 11th centuries. Behind the town the Iron-Age fortress of Castle Law was used by the Picts. Some six stones from classes I and III were found here, four of which are in **NMS Edinburgh**.

5.1: **C.I.** This was dug out of the foundations of a house *c.* 1820 and finally erected against the wall of the round tower at NO 190 164.
Front: a hammer and anvil either side of the broken sword symbol (here perhaps representing tongs); below, part of a crescent and V-rod.

5.2: ✤ **C.III. ORS.** *c.* 1 ft (31 cm) high. Fragment found in a churchyard. **NMS** IB 98.
Front: two legs of a horse above a horizontal raised band containing three Ogam letters that might read I M Q, or if read the other way round, I M N.

5.3: ✤ small fragment sculpted with a key-pattern.

5.4: ✤ **C.III. ORS.** 1 ft 8 in (51 cm) tall. Section of a broken cross-slab. **NMS** IB 255.
Front: crucified Christ from waist down with a spear and sponge-bearers either side. Below, the heads of three nuns (perhaps symbolising the three Marys at the Crucifixion).

Comment: A convent was allegedly founded here by nuns from Kildare at King Nechtan's order in the 7th century.

5.5: ✣ C.III. Sandstone. 1 ft 5 in (43 cm) long. Fragment of a cross-shaft found in a roadside wall in 1896. Sculpture is erased from the front and back. **NMS** IB 176. *Right edge:* running scroll of a stem without foliage. *Left edge:* interlace with double-beaded bands.

5.6: ✣ part of a cross-shaft found *c.*1957. **NMS** IB 290.

6 Caiplie Chapel Cave Situated off the A917 between Anstruther and Crail. NO 600 058. A Z-rod can be seen among superimposed crosses that surround it. Also an ?arch or part of a crescent in another small cave to the east.

7 Carpow ✣ C.III. ORS. 2½ft (76 cm) high. Fragment of a cross-slab found as the lintel of the well in Carpow House garden half a mile (0.8 km) north-east of Abernethy in Tayside. It is now kept in the grounds of Mugdrum House. NO 226 183.
Front: left side of the cross is defaced. Right side of the shaft, interlaced fish monsters with recessed ornamental border of spiral-work edging the cross. A round hole has been driven through the armpit and connecting ring of the two crosses on front and back. *Back:* left of the shaft, a stag – partly surrounded by a border of interlace – looks over its shoulder. Below, a ?horse with scrolled body. Traces of ornament.

8 Collessie Man, Newton Farm. **C.I.** 9 ft (274 cm) tall. This figure was discovered in 1933, incised into the top half of a Neolithic or Bronze Age monolith, standing in a field near Collessie village at NO 293 132. In 1994 it fell over but in the summer of 1995 it was re-erected on its original site.
Description: At 3¾ ft (114 cm) tall, this long-nosed naked warrior wears an interesting hair-style thought to resemble the Suebian knot described by Tacitus in Germania 38. He strides across the stone from right to left and carries a long rectangular shield held diagonally across his body in one hand and a spear with a round butt in the other. Traces of two symbols can be seen on the edge in front of the figure.

9 Crail C.III. Sandstone. 6¼ft (191 cm) tall. Very worn. ringed cross-slab used as a paving stone in Crail church after 1815. Now built into inside the wall of the tower. NO 613 080.

Front: a man carrying a cross from its base. Right of the shaft, an enthroned figure may be the Virgin holding the Child with a man (?Joseph) behind. Left of the shaft, a bird pecks at the eye of one of several beasts. Bottom centre, sunk panel bears a coat-of-arms added at later date.

10 Creich ✤ C.I. Part of a slab with relief sculpture. Found here 6½ miles (10 km) NE from Newburgh. **NMS** IB 165. **St Andrews Museum**.

11 Dogton ✤ C.III. Yellow sandstone. 5 ft (152 cm) high. Badly defaced and mutilated free-standing cross set within railings on its original base by a field wall at Dogton Farm. NT 236 968.

Back: a circular raised boss, a horseman with spear. Lower portion defaced.

Right side: two snakes biting each other with bodies interlaced at intervals.

PS: faint traces of an arch and another symbol (?Pictish beast) can just be seen round the side of the stone.

12 Dunblane Cathedral is an ancient Christian Pictish site dedicated to the 6th century St Blane. Part of the tower was built before 1100. It was restored in 1889 when two stones were recovered.

13 Dunblane

13.1: C.III. ORS. *c.* 6 ft (183 cm) tall. Ringed cross-slab.

Front: top and lower ends of a cross terminate in single spirals. Bead moulding outlining the cross ends at the foot in two serpent heads with protruding tongues.

Back: single panel reading from the top: (1) two facing beasts on hind-legs with fore-paws crossed and a single spiral in upper right corner; (2) a piece of square key-pattern surrounding square figure filled with five bosses like dots on dice; (3) a small ringed-cross on the left with a design like a key-hole plate to the right; (4) a horseman with a spear and dog; (5) a disc ornamented with a cross on the right surrounded by crude key-pattern and spirals;

(6) a man with a staff lying with his feet towards a single spiral on the right similar to the spiral on the top right of the stone.

13.2: C.III. ORS. 2¾ ft (71 cm) long. Side panel contains three pieces of ornament, ten-cord plaiting, diagonal key-pattern and zoomorphic interlace.

14 Dunino

14.1: C.III. 2½ ft (76 cm) tall. Very worn cross-slab in the churchyard which once held a sundial in 1698. Now broken off. NO 541 109.
Front and back: both sides have a crude weathered cross incised. One cross shows a saltire inside a central circle.

14.2: ✢ C.III. Cross-slab now in **St Andrews Museum**.

14.3: Dunino Den, reached by steps cut into the rock from the church above, is a magical place. The stream has carved a deep channel through the sandstone leaving a natural amphithreatre which may have been a setting for ancient rituals. Above the burn, a basin – *c.* 4 ft (122 cm) by 2 ft (61 cm) – deliberately cut out of the rock is usually filled with rain water. When visited in May, this was decorated with posies of wild hyacinths which grow in profusion everywhere. At one side of this basin a foot-print has been hollowed out of the rock. At the bottom of the steps and 40 yd (37 m) along a modern path find a magnificent carving of a ringed cross some 9 ft (274 cm) tall and 6 ft (183 cm) across incised high on the cliff over-looking the den. This may be a typical example of a pagan ritual site converted to Christianity by the presence of the cross. The rock-basin and footprint recall Dunadd (Argyll) where kings of Dal Riata were crowned. The amphithreatre could have held hundreds of people gathered to watch the ceremony.

15 East Lomond Hill ✢ C.I. Yellow sandstone. Discovered *c.* 1920 within the south side of the fort at NO 244 062. **NMS** IB 205.
PS: a bull.

16 The East Wemyss Caves are located on the shore-line of East Wemyss village some 5 miles (8 km) NE of Kirkcaldy. Some have Pictish symbols carved on the walls and, though many have been tampered with, others remain as they were. The problem here is erosion, but recently Kirkcaldy District Council and local pressure groups such as Save the Wemyss Caves (SWACS) have taken the matter to heart and are building up and repairing the old paths.

From West to East they can be located as follows:

16.1: The Court Cave had eight recognisable symbols including two double-discs, a mirror and crescent & V-rod. A figure with a spear can still be seen, but with difficulty, among the many doodles and graffiti. NT 343 970.

16.2: The Dovecot Cave had twelve symbols, but the crescent & V-rod and animal head were in that part of the cave which has more or less collapsed. NT 343 970.

16.3: The Well Caves have no symbols.

16.4: Jonathan's Cave still has the greatest number of symbols recognisable today, including an excellent boat with oars which may be Pictish rather than Norse. Casts of the carvings from this cave and the **Court Cave** may be seen in **NMS Edinburgh** and also in **Kirkcaldy Museum**. NT 345 972.

16.5 The Sliding or Sloping Cave still shows most of the symbols seen a century ago including a rectangle and double-disc. NT 346 973.

17 Falkland Palace ✤ Two **C.I** stones cut into building blocks, found when part of Westfield Farm was demolished in 1971. NO 238 073. Now in **NTS** Museum at **Falkland Place**.
PS on **17.1:** disc and rectangle set horizontally left of part of a vertical double-disc.
PS on **17.2:** two concentric arches and notched rectangle.

18 Hawkhill C.III. 8½ ft (251 cm) tall. Cross-slab which bears long incised crosses on the front and back. It may have been a tombstone, for when the site was excavated in 1829 many human bones were found, including a stone cist containing bones and with crosses cut into both ends of covering flag. Half a mile (0.8 km) east of Alloa in Clackmannan-shire. NS 902 926.

19 Inchcolm Island ✤
19.1: C.III. Sandstone. 2 ft 2 in (66 cm) tall. Fragment of a

cross broken off at top and sculptured in relief on the front and left side in diagonal key-pattern and interlace. Firth of Forth. NT 190 826. A recent dig failed to find it. Lost.

19.2: recumbent hogback sandstone monument which stood on a hill west of the Abbey and has recently been moved into the Visitor's Centre to prevent further weathering.

20 Inverkeithing Stone ✢ C.III. 10 ft (305 cm) tall. Cross-slab which once stood in the north of parish. It disappeared between 1845 and 56, and is now firmly lost. It was first mentioned in 1726 when sketched by a Sandy Gordon. J. Stewart while researching *The Sculptured Stones of Scotland* in 1856, included the sketch in this book.
  Description: thought to have had five panels on back; (1) a horseman facing left; (2) two horsemen facing left; (3) a beast chasing a man; (4) a beast with three pairs of crossed legs and seal-like head.
  Comment: a recent reproduction by Leslie Alan Reid may be seen in Abbot House, Dunfermline Heritage Trust, Maygate, Dunfermline.

21 Kilrenny ✢ C.II or C.III. Dark red sandstone. Fragment of a large ringed cross-slab found in 1993 among a heap of dumped material in an eroding area of the beach at NO 580 043. Now in **Crail Museum**, Market Street, Crail.
  Front: the top arm and part of the right side and central medallion are decorated. The top right corner of the upper arm is expanded by an external spiral.

22 Kilrenny, Upper (Skeith Stone) C.III. Whinstone. 4 ft (193 cm) tall. Unusually shaped cross set in a ring within which are eight lozenge-shaped depressions arranged in pairs to form the cross. Find it on the field boundary at NO 572 046.

23 Largo C.II. ORS. 6½ ft (198 cm) tall. Very worn cross-slab found in two pieces, one of which covered a drain in 1839. It has been moved to many sites since then, and eventually returned to a shelter in the gateway of Largo Parish Church. A new shelter is currently under consideration. NO 423 035.
  Front: a ringed equal-armed cross on a long shaft raised on a rectangular base. The decoration is

mostly gone. On the right of the shaft, two interlaced seahorses face and touch each other.
Back: three mounted hunters with two hounds. Left of the two lower horsemen find a double-disc & Z-rod. Below, a Pictish beast with 2 ?deer.

24 Lindores (or Abdie) **C.I.** Greenstone. 3 ft (91 cm) high. This once stood on the crest of Kaimhill. It was moved to Old Mort House (Abdie Churchyard) and is now in Abdie Church. NO 259 163.
PS: a cauldron above a decorated double-disc & Z-rod with a mirror on the right edge.
Comment: The stone also bears a sundial and below it an OS bench mark in the centre of the double-disc.

25 Mugdrum ✣ **C.III.** Sandstone. 11 ft (335 cm) high. Very mutilated free-standing cross, still on its original base, near Newburgh in the grounds of Mugdrum House at NO 225 180.
Front: cross arms both missing. Shaft has four panels; (1) and (2) a man on horseback; (3) two men on horseback one with a spear; (4) several hounds attacking badly defaced beasts with interlaced legs.
Back and left side: almost entirely defaced.
Right side: two panels of scroll foliage with diagonal key-pattern below.

26 Sauchope C.III. Sandstone. 6 ft (183 cm) tall. Cross-slab, which formerly stood on the mound west of Sauchope House near Fife Ness, it is now in Crail's public park at NO 611 079.
Front: undecorated cross. Background below shaft, two beasts.
Back: two horsemen, one with a spear and dog.

27 Scoonie ✣ **C.II.** Sandstone. 3½ ft (107 cm) tall. Cross-slab, partly incised, partly carved in relief. It was found in the old parish church at NO 384 017. **NMS** IB 110.
Front: cross has all but disappeared.
Back: Pictish beast above hunting scene with three riders and at least three beasts. Ogam inscription on vertical stem right of hunters reads E D D A R R N O N.

28 Strathmiglo C.I. This was found in use as a gate-post which had fallen and was re-erected in the local church-yard at NO 218 102.

PS: a disc with notched rectangle, a beast head.

29 Tulliebole ✣ Kinross-shire. **C.III.** *c.* 10th century. 4 ft 3 in (130 cm) tall. This was found in the 1870s at the old burial ground at Tulliebole Castle, owned by the Moncrieffes, at NO 054 008. **NMS** IB 99.
Front: a very worn cross with spiral extensions to the arms, decorated with six-cord plait-work. Background right of the shaft, a panel with diagonal key-pattern.
Back: divided into four panels showing from the top (1) a man on foot with right hand raised and a man on horseback above what looks like another horse and hound; (2) two circular discs; (3) bottom left, two men wrestling and (4) bottom right, two serpents with looped tails facing each other.
Comment: a Hogback stone was uncovered in the same graveyard in 1989.

30 Walton C.I. ORS. Fragment found on Walton Farm near Springfield, close to the site of a fort at NO 363 096. Preserved at nearby Crawford Priory and a cast presented to **NMS** IB 175 in 1894. When examined in 1971 there were doubts as to its authenticity.

31 West Lomond Hill EC. A small ringed cross found in 1992 on Balharvie Moss at NO 202 071.
Front: a fish incised above a cross. Thought to be EC *ichthus* (Greek word for fish symbol taken from the first letters for Christ's name *Iesous Christos Theou Uios Soter).* The EC fish is rare in Scotland and Ireland. The Fife Regional Archaeologist suggests the stone may have been a shrine used by travellers and could date from any time between the 7th and 10th centuries.

32 West Lomond Hill Stone with an incised Pictish beast visible beside a high track at NO 223 078 was carved recently with a 6-inch (15 cm) nail by Leslie Alan Reid. Nice but not authentic.

Pictish sites without stones

33 Norries Law NO 409 073. Tumulus in Largo Estate where not less than 400 oz (12.5 kg) of decorated silver was discovered in 1819. Much of it disappeared, much was melted down, but much still survives including two silver plaques decorated with red enamel and displaying a double-disc & Z-rod with beast-head symbols to be seen in **NMS**. The hoard was thought to have been hidden in the second half of the 7th century AD during the conquest of Fife by the Northumbrians.

34 Clatchard Craig, Fife. NO 243 178. Inland fortress destroyed this century by quarrying after detailed excavation.

35 Dumyat, Stirlingshire. NS 832 973. Stronghold thought to have been a major fortress of the Maeatae Picts.

36 Myothill, near Denny, Stirlingshire. NS 782 825. This is thought to have been the southern outpost of the Maeatae Picts. The whole area has been so industrialised over the past that any stones which may have been erected here have possibly been disregarded, broken or lost centuries ago.

AROUND
PERTHSHIRE

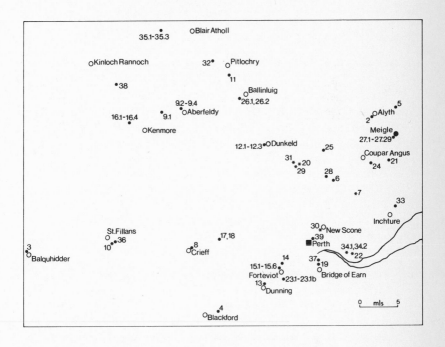

35.1-35.3 ○Blair Atholl

○Kinloch Rannoch   32● ○Pitlochry

●38   ●11

                                    ●Ballinluig
                    9.2-9.4   ●26.1,26.2
16.1-16.4   ●9.1 ○Aberfeldy   2●○Alyth ●5
            ○Kenmore   Meigle
                                                        27.1-27.29●
                        12.1-12.3 ●○Dunkeld   ●25
                                31●   ●20   ○Coupar Angus
                                29●   28 ●24 ●21
                                        ●6
                                            ●7   ●33
                                                        ○Inchture
        St.Fillans   30●○New Scone
        ○   ●17,18   ●39
        10●●36   ■Perth 34.1,34.2
3   ●8   ● ●22
○Balquhidder   ○Crieff   37●
                            14   ●19
                15.1-15.6● ○Bridge of Earn
                Forteviot○ ●23.1-23.1b
                13○
                ○Dunning
        ●4
        ○Blackford   0   mls   5

1 Perth Museum, George Street, has a fine collection of stones, including the massive St Madoe's cross-slab, with the Inchyra, Gellyburn and New Scone stones all described on their sites. An earlier round stone carved with four human heads found in a wall at Glenfoot, Abernethy would seem to represent the Celtic cult of the head while a small Bronze-Age cup-marked boulder with an EC cross on the the back was found at Shenavail, Dull. Unfortunately St Madoe's stone is disappointingly displayed with the back reflected in a mirror which makes it extremely hard to interpret. Considering the importance of this cross-slab I believe it should be better placed within the museum.

OPEN: All the year from l0 am – 5 pm, except on Sundays and public holidays.

2 Alyth C.II. Greenish slate or gneiss. 4½ ft (137 cm) tall. Cross-slab found in 1887 by the minister's servant while levelling ground in front of the manse. Now in the church at NO 243 488.
Front: Latin cross with spike at the bottom set near the top of the stone. The background of the decorated cross contains four single spirals.
Back: part of a double disc & Z-rod. The remaining disc is decorated like a spoked wheel.

3 Balquhidder C.III. 5 ft (152 cm) and 4½ ft (137 cm). Two cross-slabs in a remote little church. Both show incised crosses. (N.M. Robertson has recently found four medieval crosses lying in the churchyard.) NN 535 209.

4 Blackford, Peterhead Farm. **C.I.** Two stones, one with PS and the other with no designs, found on the farm between Blackford and Gleneagles at NN 924 098.
PS: a goose or (considering its site) an eagle and rectangle.

5 Bruceton C.I. 4 ft 6 in (137 cm) high. This stands in a field 3-4 miles (5 to 6.5 km) north-east of Alyth, 100 yds (100 m) from the River Isla, which formed the ancient boundary between Forfarshire and Perthshire at NO 290 504.
PS: an arch above a Pictish beast.

6 Cargill ✛ **C.I.** Whinstone. 3 ft (91 cm) high. This used to stand in a field at Balholmie House and is now in the rockery. NO 148 362.

PS: a rectangle incised on a vertical line like a spade beside a larger variant of rectangle.

7 Collace, Fairy Green. ❖ **C.I.** Metamophosed sandstone. This was found in 1948 buried in a field at NO 207 332 and is now in the **Anthropological Museum, Aberdeen University.**
PS: a Pictish Beast, mirror and comb, rectangle.

8 Crieff Cross-slab **C.III.** Indurated sandstone. 6¼ ft (190 cm) tall. This stands in the High Street on the east side of the River Earn. NN 868 217.
Front: eight panels filled with defaced interlace.
Back: all sculpture defaced.
Left edge: key-pattern at the top with foliage below.
Right edge: foliage at the top and diagonal key-pattern below.

9 Dull Church
9.1 ❖ **C.III.** Yellow sandstone. 2¾ ft (84 cm) high. Broken. It was found before 1900 when digging grave in churchyard at NN 806 492. **NMS** IB 58.
Front: an important-looking rider in the centre with a collared dog followed by half a similar figure also with a collared dog. On the left find busts of two men facing riders and below them three foot soldiers with pleated and hemmed tunics wearing bossed shields.

9.2, 9.3, 9.4: C.III. *c.* 6 ft (152 cm) high. Two of these free-standing crosses are in Weem Church, the other is in the kirkyard. Dull may have been a monastic site. NN 806 592.

10 Dundurn EC. This was found recently by N.M. Robertson in the kirkyard of the old church dedicated to St Fillan which stands below the royal fortress of Dundurn at NN 703 235.

11 Dunfallandy C.II. Cross-slab recognised in 1856 in the ruins of the old chapel near Killiecrankie. It was erected before 1900 behind Dunfallandy Cottage on the west bank of the River Tummel just south of Pitlochry at NN 946 565.
Front: an equal-armed cross on a long shaft divided into seven panels of varied and finely carved interlace. The top and bottom arms contain five bosses with the side arms holding three each (perhaps symbolising the five wounds of Christ and the Trinity).

The background is filled with nine panels, including two seraphs, a centaur, deer and four fantastic beasts. The bottom left panel shows a dragon with wings, claws and fish tail swallowing or regurgitating a pair of human legs (?Jonah and the whale).

Back: framed with two fish-tailed serpents whose heads meet in the top centre holding a human head between their tongues. Below, two enthroned figures linked by a small cross with the Pictish beast above the head of the left-hand person and a double-disc and crescent & V-rod above the larger figure on the right. Below centre, a mounted monk with double-disc and Pictish beast in front of his horse. Below again, the hammer, anvil and tongs of the black-smith's profession. Note the lower carvings are incised, while upper motifs are in relief.

Comment: N.M. Robertson suggests that the two enthroned figures are husband and wife, linked in Christian marriage, each with their lineage symbols above them. Below, their clerical son displays his inherited symbols in front of him. The iron symbols below may show the family profession. ECMS interprets the enthroned figures as Moses and Elias, with the cross as symbol of Christ at the Transfiguration. You can see the cloud that enveloped them between the top symbols. Perhaps both interpretations are valid. The head held by the serpents may symbolise the soul of the mounted monk elevated to heaven.

Dunkeld was a royal site in Pictish times. Relics of Columba were brought here by Kenneth Mac Alpin in the 9th century and it became the seat of an abbot who was also the most important bishop at the time when Picts and Scots were united.

12 Dunkeld

12.1: C.II or C.III. Grey sandstone. 3½ ft (107 cm) long. This was found embedded in the King's Park at NO 023 426 and is now to be seen in the tower of Dunkeld Cathedral.

Right end: a horseman with spear and horn.

12.2: C.III. Grey sandstone. *c.* 5 ft (152 cm). A carved slab once used as a gate-post to the churchyard entrance before being taken into cathedral. Busy, complicated and weathered.

Front: probably the remains of a cross but indecipherable. Two horsemen at the top, and a row of four pedestrians underneath. Below, three prostrate men, one beheaded, also a man with hands raised in prayer surrounded by four beasts, probably Daniel in the lions' den (*see* Meigle 27.1). At the foot, six men in a row with haloes. Two recessed panels on either side of centre show beasts; the creature on the right is remarkably like an elephant.

Back: three panels as follows; (1) at the top find 16 or more figures and a circular disc (This might represent the Miracle of the Loaves and Fishes or Israelites crossing the Red Sea with the chariot wheel.); (2) and (3) show two rows of six men which may represent the 12 apostles or the 12 tribes of Israel.

Right edge: a mounted man above a larger figure with nimbus who stands beside what might be a small section of the right arm of a cross. At the foot three men face outwards.

Left edge: defaced.

12.3: ✣ **C.III.** Fragments of a cross-slab used as a tombstone for a farmer in 1729 and afterwards as part of the cathedral pavement floor. Lost since 1900.

13 Dunning C.III. Sandstone. Nearly 4 ft (122 cm) long. Cross-slab found before 1900 and kept in Dunning church at NO 019 145.

Front: each side shows an equal-armed ringed cross with rounded armpits but no ornamentation.

Right and left edges: portion of four-cord plaitwork.

14 Dupplin Cross C.III. ORS. 8½ ft (259 cm) tall and 3 ft (91 cm) across the arms. Free-standing cross in Cross Park field at NO 051 189. Although the Pictish era was probably over when the stone was carved in the 9th or 10th centuries, Pictish expertise was surely responsible for its fine elaborate design.

Front: the head of the cross is surrounded by roll-moulding which makes spiral curves at intervals with a raised circular boss in the centre, which has ribbed border containing cross. Shaft is divided into three panels; (1) once thought impossible to decipher is now (after casting) to be read as a Latin inscription which translates CUSTANTIN SON OF WUIRGUST (Constantin Mac Fergus); (2) four pairs of birds with their beaks and legs crossed and interlaced round a raised boss full of circular interlace; (3) David rending the lion's jaw with two other beasts.

Left side: three small panels of interlace on top with three panels down side of shaft; (1) an elaborate beast biting its own tail; (2) a man seated on chair playing a large triangular harp (maybe David as psalmist and musician); (3) six-cord plait-work.

Back: similar moulding round the cross as on front but the pattern within the central boss is much defaced. The arms are filled with scrolled foliage while at the top find a panel of diagonal key-pattern. Three panels on the shaft, separated by key-pattern, show (1) a warrior with a spear on horseback; (2) four foot soldiers with spears and shields – maybe young elite recruits; (3) a hound leaping on a ?hind.

Right edge: four panels of varied interlace with three panels down the edge of the shaft; (2) a pair of dog-like beasts on their haunches with front paws embracing; (2) two foot soldiers with shields strapped round their necks, holding spears. Their tunic hems are embroidered; (3) some knot-work.

Comment: Dr Michael Spearman at the **NMS** suggests that Dupplin might have been erected by Kenneth Mac Alpin or one of his sons as a suitable dedication to a Pictish king (Constantine mac Fergus) who, like Kenneth himself, had once ruled both the Picts and the Scots with their best interests at heart.

15 Forteviot Six **C.III** stones have been found in this important royal capital of the Pictish kingdom, the palace of which was approximately one mile south-west of Dupplin at NO 052 175, where the stones are in the church.

15.1: C.III. Sandstone. 2 ft (61 cm) tall. Lower part of a cross-slab, broken off at the top, sculpted on both sides and edges.

Front: variety of interlace.

Back: the lower parts of two beasts with hind-legs meeting in lower centre. The tail of the beast on the right turns into the knotted body of a serpent which appears to be biting the horn of a beast which is biting the serpent at the back of its head.

Right edge: plaited tails of three creatures touch the head of a man.

Left edge: interlace and triangular interlace.

15.2: Forteviot Arch ✣ Sandstone. 6½ ft (198 cm) long, 1½ ft (46 cm) deep by *c.* 1 ft (30 cm) thick. This was probably the top of a doorway decorated on one face only. Was displayed in **NMS** (IB 36) over the entrance to the Dark Age Room. Superbly carved.

Front: an equal-armed cross on a pedestal, badly defaced in the centre. Left of the cross, a large seated figure with curled hair and long moustaches is holding a sword with both hands across his thighs while his feet rest on a small beast. Could this be Kenneth mac Alpin himself? Right of the cross, is a lamb with a solemn expression touching the cross with its hoof (Agnus Dei, perhaps). To the right, two men, possibly part of a third, in fine robes and holding staves face away from the lamb.

15.3: fragment of the arm of an outline cross decorated with triangular interlace with double-beaded bands. The left edge is also decorated.

15.4: fragment of a cross-slab showing a man on horseback with a spear.

15.5: fragment sculpted with interlace on one side.

15.6: ✣ Lost.

Comment: the church is involved in raising a restoration appeal for a large sum of money to bring it back to a state worthy of its great historic past.

16 Fortingall has four stones, all found in walls during demolition of a pre-Reformation church *c.* 1900, now seen on the window-sills of the present church. A further stone with a cross marks the threshold to the church gate. NN 742 471 some 7 miles (11 km) west of Dull.

16.1: Grey sandstone. 1 ft 8 in (51 cm) tall, upper part of a cross-slab broken into three pieces.

Front: ringed-cross ornamented on the shaft and arms with six-cord plait-work and spirals with key-pattern in the background to the right of the shaft.

Back: portions of clothing of two ecclesiastics.

Edges: key-pattern.

16.2: small fragment of a cross-slab decorated on both sides.

16.3: two fragments of a cross-slab joined together and decorated on the front only.

16.4: top part of a cross-slab broken off on three sides and sculptured on the front only.

Front: cross-slab with circular depressions in the angles ornamented with two-cord plait-work and with triquetra knots at the endings. Another triquetra can be seen in the upper right corner.

17 Fowlis Wester C.II. ORS. 10¼ ft (315 cm) tall. Weathered cross-slab which, until recently, stood in Fowlis Wester village within iron railings and with an iron chain attached to the centre top. NN 928 240. Now inside the parish church with a replica of sorts on its original site.

Front: side arms of a cross extend beyond the slab. Central panel displays eight raised bosses arranged in a circle around central boss. Key pattern on the four equal arms. At the foot of the long shaft find traces of birds and beasts.

Back: from the top, find a double-disc, horsemen, beast, two further horsemen riding abreast, one carrying a hawk, cow with a bell round its neck led by man in long tunic and followed by procession of six more men, two of whom seem to be carrying square shields or maybe ?buckets, crescent & V-rod with a bird (?eagle), and at the bottom, a man being eaten by monster.

Comment: the cow leading the six men may refer to the worship of the Golden Calf or it may relate to some seasonal festivity and have a local significance long forgotten.

18 Fowlis Wester Church C.III (as far as we know). This cross-slab is inside the church, set so close to the wall that the back cannot be seen.

Front: ringed cross set on a square base consisting of five panels filled with knot-work, plait-work and spirals. Top background left is the whale which swallowed Jonah with his shield and sword. Right top background, the whale regurgitates Jonah. The reluctant prophet from the Old Testament Book of Jonah prefigures Christ and his Resurrection.

Below, on either side of shaft, find two hermits, Anthony and Paul, as described by St Jerome in the 3rd century. Anthony enthroned on the right is being prompted by an angel to visit Paul, who is also enthroned on a grander chair on the left with the date palm trees that fed him in the wilderness.

Below Paul, find two tonsured and elaborately vested monks.

19 The Boar Stone of *Gask* ✤ C.II. ORS. 6¼ ft (191 cm) tall. Ringed cross-slab. This once stood in field on the road-side near Gask House at NO 133 193. Around 1900, it was moved to Moncrieffe House at NO 136 193.
Front: a cross badly mutilated with holes pierced through the lower arm-pits. The right and upper arms are broken away. Faint traces of interlace are visible on the shaft. The background is filled with unrecognisable figures.
Back: a cross similar to the front, but with spiral terminations to the horizontal arms. Circular interlace on the shaft is also obliterated. The left side of the shaft is crammed with fabulous creatures, including two centaurs, a bug-eyed long-horned male beast and small beast above its back, and a creature brandishing the head of a similar beast at the end of its tail and finally some interlace. The background to the right of the shaft shows a beast swallowing a serpent, two boar-like creatures with raised ridges and tails between their legs, a snake & Z-rod, horseman with flower symbol above another horseman with small beast to the right of his head, ?dog.

20 Gellyburn, Murthly. ✤ **C.II.** Broken cross-slab found in a house wall in 1949 at NO 094 392. **Perth Museum.**
Front: a cross.
Back: a roundel, crescent & V-rod, a Pictish beast.

21 High Keillor C.I. Grey gneiss. 6¼ ft (191 cm) tall. This stands on the north slope of Hill of Keillor some 444 ft (135 m) above sea level at NO 273 397.
PS: a beast resembling a wolf or bear but much more like a badger or even a wolverine, a double-disc & Z-rod.

22 Inchyra ✤ C.I. This was found by the plough in 1945, and was one of several slabs covering an inhumation burial at NO 190 212. **Perth Museum.**
One side: a double-disc and salmon, broken sword and unfinished mirror with Ogam inscription at the top.
Other side: a salmon and snake.

23 Invermay House ✤ C.III. Situated about 2 miles (3 km) south of Forteviot at NO 067 161 once had a cross-slab in the grounds which was deliberately broken up and the fragments thrown away as rubbish into a field sometime before 1890. Three fragments were allegedly saved.

23.1: part of a panel with plait-work.

23.1a and **23.1b:** narrow band of beading at the top with a diagonal key pattern in the centre and at the bottom the edge of a similar panel.

24 Kettins C.III. ORS. 9 ft 2 in (279 cm) tall. Cross-slab used as a footbridge across the Kettins burn and erected in the churchyard on the north side close to the boundary wall at NO 238 391.
Front: a very defaced cross with only three patches of pattern remaining. To the right of the shaft find four indistinct panels; (1) a beast with tail curled over its back; (2) a winged griffin holding something in its mouth; (3) a man in a cloak with two beast-masked men either side; (4) two beasts with crossed bodies biting each other's tails.

25 Lethendy Tower ✤ has a 10th-century Picto/Scottish stone panel built into the underside of one of the stone steps of the spiral stair in the older part of the house at NO 141 417.
Front: an angel above two seated monks and, below, two standing musicians. The one on the left plays a triangular harp with heavy soundbox and seven strings similar to Monifeith 29.4. The figure on the right plays a triple pipe the lowest pipe of which is longer and seems larger than the others. Between the two musicians is a ?barrel-drum with the head inverted. Below find (possibly) a cat.

26 Logierait
26.1: C.III. Whinstone. *c.* 4 ft (122 cm) tall. Cross-slab broken at the top in Logierait churchyard at NN 968 520.
Front: a decorated cross with central medallion and four raised bosses in rounded armpits. Spiral terminations at the foot of the shaft.
Back: part of a horseman with spear. The horse wears a detailed bridle and fringed saddle blanket. Below, a serpent twined around a ?sceptre.

26.2: C.II. Found in a churchyard by N.M. Robertson in 1989. Now in the parish church at NN 968 520.

Front: a ringed cross flanked with interlace and beasts above the upper arms.
Back: badly weathered. Shows a double-disc and serpent & Z-rod, a dog and parts of two horses.

27 Meigle Museum

The old Meigle Church must have been an important Christian centre in the 8th-10th centuries. Apart from the presence of so many stones, there is evidence of a scribe called Thana who visited Meigle around 840, and who is said to have written the early history of St Andrews. The Museum at NO 287 446 was once the old schoolhouse where, *c.* 1900, under the direction of Sir George Kinloch, most of the stones were gathered after the church was burned down. In 1936 the building and its collection came under the care of the state now known as Historic Scotland.

OPEN: April–September, 9.30 am–6 pm on weekdays: lunch break 12.30–1.30 pm: Sundays, 2–6 pm. Closed October–March.

27.1 ❖ C.II. ORS. 6¼ft (191 cm) tall. Cross-slab which was once a prehistoric monolith, with Bronze-Age cup-marks, re-used by the Picts.

Front: a long-shafted ringed cross with round hollow armpits, divided into seven linked panels of assorted interlace. The background is divided into eight panels all containing animals, real and fantastic. Top left and right are two snouted creatures like boars. Left of the shaft from the top; a goat-like beast, a snouted beast with interlaced body, a seahorse and similar fish-tailed creature facing each other. Right of the shaft, a pair of interlaced seahorses. Below, a horned animal biting its own serpent-headed tail.

Back: a single panel with scattered motifs reading from the top; a large salmon, a small beast's head symbol, a small triquetra and tiny Pictish beast above a large snake & Z-rod and small horned beast with legs doubled beneath it. A large mirror & double-edged comb, a group of five horsemen and a hound; an angel with spread wings. To the right under the comb, a camel-like beast and reptile with coiled body and two heads.

The Daniel Stone or **Meigle 27.2 ❖ C.III. ORS.** *c.* 8 ft (244 cm) tall. Magnificent rectangular cross-slab with a projection at each side.

Front: a ringed cross set with 33 raised bosses in the centre, arms and ring. The shaft shows three pairs of beasts set vertically, but too defaced for description. Left background; three climbing men with the first hauling the second up to his perch between the shaft and ring. Right background; three beasts with large heads and long contorted bodies.

Back: a single panel with four motifs; (1) top, a spirited hunter – perhaps a king – with four mounted companions, two hounds and a tiny angel (perhaps symbolising the king's soul). Note that the two horsemen ride parallel (*See* Hilton of Cadboll in **NMS**.); (2) below, a splendid Daniel, hands outstretched in ancient pose of prayer, surrounded by four friendly lions and two tiny cubs (Daniel is seen as a prefiguration of Christ in that his time in the lions' den matched Christ's three days in the tomb.); (3) a centaur with two axes and the healing branch (thought to symbolise Christ the healer) and below, a man with a club or wearing a yoke, behind a dragon which seizes a bull-like creature by its head.

27.3: ✤ C.II. ORS. 1⅓ ft (11 cm) high. Upper part of a cross-slab.

Front: cross shows four panels with key-work in its arms and a triple spiral in the centre. Half a double disc in the left background.

Back: a compact armed mounted warrior with elegant tongued shoes, seated on a striped saddle blanket. Note the details of the reins and bridle.

27.4: ✤ C.II. ORS. *c.* 5 ft (152 cm) tall. A cross-slab found in 1858, broken in two pieces. The lower middle section is missing.

Upper front: cross with five panels of assorted designs. Upper background, the bodies of two fantastic beasts form a border around the stone (*see* Dunfallandy). Right background of the shaft, a man seizes a horse by the right foreleg. Left background, a small seahorse and interlace.

Lower front: the foot of decorated shaft with zoomorphic designs in background.

Upper back: single panel. At the top left, an armed horseman on a huge saddle-blanket. Note the horse's pricked ears and high-stepping foreleg. Top right, a pair of interlaced serpents. Below, from left, a Pictish

beast above the top edge of crescent & V-rod, four-legged beast biting the tail of an interlaced serpent above and, squashed against the right border, a smaller horse with a similar high-stepping foreleg and rider.
Lower back: fantastic interlaced beasts.

27.5: ✧ C.II. ORS. 2½ ft (76 cm) high. Cross-slab with the right corner missing.
Front: a border of interlace frames three edges of elegant equal-armed linked cross with elaborate base that rears up into two beasts' heads on each side. The background is divided into three panels, the fourth is missing; (1) top left, a beast with a long crest biting its back; (2) left of the shaft, a goggle-eyed bird monster and (3) a bird swallowing a serpent.
Back: a headless horseman wearing tongued shoes seated on a striped saddle-blanket set in recessed panel.
Left edge: an incised disc and rectangle above a Pictish beast.

27.6: ✧ C.II. ORS. 1 ft 10 in (56 cm) tall. Middle part of a cross-slab.
Front: diagonal key-pattern in the cross-shaft.
Back: a border of diagonal key-pattern surrounds a headless horseman with bossed shield and sword, an ornamented double-disc and crescent both without rods, above leaping hound.

27.7: ✧ C.II. ORS. 1½ ft (46 cm) high. Rounded top portion of a cross-slab.
Front: Top part of a cross filled with diagonal key-pattern. Top left background shows a crouching man holding the left edge of the cross's upper arm while a rampant beast fills the top right background.
Back: a single panel with a double-disc & Z-rod above a ?double-sided comb and perhaps part of a mirror.

27.8: ✧ C.II.? ORS. Under 1 ft (30 cm). Fragment of a cross-slab.
Front: unique symbol of a circle attached to two horizontal bars and intersected by a vertical line. Below, the heads of two ?pigs facing each other with paws in each other's mouths.

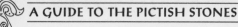

27.9: ✣ C.III. Sandstone. *c.* 6 ft (183 cm) long. Recumbent monument with a socket for an upright cross near the head of the stone.

Front side: five panels reading left to right, (1) a beast; (2) a swan-like bird with a long neck curved round the head of a seated man who seems to be holding one leg which is interlaced with the man's limbs and lower body. Note the bird's webbed foot; (3) a beast with defaced head; (4) partly defaced spirals; (5) traces of defaced men.

Back: divided into four panels; (1) a griffin carrying a beast; (2) traces of interlace; (3) a beast with its body interlaced; (4) two beasts sharing a head.

27.10: ✣ C.III. Sandstone. 3 ft (91 cm) long by 1½ ft (46 cm) high. Slab mutilated, possibly to make building block. Lost.

Front: three men in an elevated chariot drawn by pair of parallel horses with a dog? Below the chariot, a kneeling archer shoots at the back of a retreating beast which confronts a huge fanged beast in the act of devouring a prone and naked man. In the top right corner, hindquarters of a beast with its tail between its legs. (Dr J. Anderson suggested the scene represented the Ascension of Elijah.)

27.11: ✣ C.III. Sandstone. 5 ft 5 in (165 cm) long at the top and longer at the bottom. Recumbent monument sculptured on four sides with a socket for an upright cross-slab.

Front: inside a raised margin, three horsemen process in row, the first accompanied by a hound and the third followed by a man with a beast head holding interlaced serpents.

Back: a single panel within a raised margin contains two interlaced beasts, a fat creature with two smaller animals above and below. A grid of 12 raised bosses with spirals, a circle of seven bosses surrounded by two monsters with a horizontal man's body pulled between their teeth.

Head end: traces of interlace.

Foot end: a lozenge-shaped figure recessed.

27.12: ✣ C.III. Sandstone. 4⅔ ft (142 cm) long. Recumbent slab with a socket for an upright cross damaged at both ends.

Top: a row of recessed lozenges within a border of interlace.

Front: a fish-monster with a long body and four pairs of fins.

Back: from the left, a beast bites the hind leg of a stag, two horned bulls confront each other.

27.13: ✤ Fragment of sandstone broken along all four edges decorated with a key-pattern and a crouching beast. Lost.

27.14: ✤ Fragment of sandstone under 1 ft (30 cm), showing the lower part of two human figures. Lost.

27.15: ✤ C.III. Sandstone. Under 1 ft (30 cm). Lower part of cross-slab. Lost.

Front: shaft interlaced. Left background, two beasts biting each other. Right background, a beast bites its own back.

27.16: ✤ Sandstone fragment under 1 ft (30 cm) high showing part of mounted warrior. Lost.

27.17: ✤ C.III. Under 1 ft (30 cm) high. Upper part of a cross-slab.

Front: the top arm of an interlaced cross. Left background, a seated beast and on the right a beast with feet doubled up beneath its body. Lost.

27.18: ✤ C.III. Sandstone. Under 1 ft (30 cm). Part of the left side of a cross-slab. The left arm of the cross is interlaced. Lost.

27.19: ✤ C.III. Sandstone. 1¼ ft (38 cm) high. Upper part of a cross-slab with pedimented top. A cross filled with five panels of assorted key-pattern and spirals. Lost.

27.20: ✤ Fragment of sandstone broken at both ends. 1 ft 7 in (48 cm) tall. Ornamented with panel of diagonal key-pattern.

27. 21: ✤ C.III. Sandstone. 2½ ft (76 cm) tall. Cross-slab.

Front: a linked cross, containing two varieties of pattern.

27.22: ✤ C.III. Sandstone. 2⅔ ft (81 cm) long. Slab fractured along two edges. It may be an architectural fragment.

Front: a strange little creature, perhaps a triton, mermaid or Celtic forest god, Cernunnos of the Groves, holds its long curls of hair in both hands. Its legs are interlaced and end in fish tails. On the left, find a beast with claws or toes and coiled trunk (?elephant) while on the right, an animal like a lioness (?dog) sleeps with its head on its forepaws.

27.23: ✤ **C.III.** Sandstone. 2 ft 7 in (79 cm) tall. Cross-slab with stepped top.

Front: a ringed cross without ornament. On each side of the shaft find small human figures.

Back: a single panel with a pair of beasts sharing the same head (*see* Meigle 29.9) above two beasts with necks twisted together looking backwards.

27.24: ✤ **C.III.** Sandstone. *c.*1 ft (30 cm) high. Cross-slab broken along two edges. Lost.

Front: the lower part of the cross is divided into three panels of assorted interlace. Left background, part of a monk with a book-satchel wearing a vestment with embroidered hem and neat shoes. On the right find two ornamented discs.

27.25: ✤ Ornamented hog-back gravestone.

27.26: ✤ **C.III** (?II). **ORS.** 5 ft (152 cm) long. Recumbent monument.

Top: socket for an upright cross at the head of the slab held within the jaws of two serpents, whose decorated bodies form a border down the edges to merge with the bodies of two birds whose beaks meet at the centre bottom. Between these borders, from the socket down, find (1) three serpents coiled into a spiral; (2) square panel crossed with a saltire with three bosses in each triangle (see Groam House saltire that displays triquetras in triangles); and (3) two seahorses with fish-tails and linked paws.

Right side: reading from the left find (1) two fantastic beasts, (2) a neat grid of square key-pattern and (3) a row of two hounds and five horsemen.

Head end: a beast with a human head – ?fabulous man-eating manticora – pursuing a naked bearded man, who looks back fearfully over his shoulder.

Left side: a stunning panel showing, from the left, two fiercesome creatures devouring the leg of a dismembered human body. (?Bestiary hyenas); (2) a group of four squatting men holding each other's feet arranged in a swastika; (3) two beasts, one a hyena, face a swastika, and behind it, a horse with its legs doubled up beneath its body. All the beasts have scrolled joints as on Burghead bulls.

27.27: ✤ **C.III.** Sandstone. 1 ft 10 in (56 cm) tall, shaped

like a polygon. Fragment of a cross-slab.
Front: part of the shaft is ornamented with spiral-work. Panels of plait-work and triangular interlace in the right background.
Back: portions of two enthroned clerics facing left. The chair of the central figure tilts backwards and behind it crouches a bearded man either on the floor or a stool, with his arms clasped round his knees.

27.28: ✣ C.III. Sandstone. 1 ft 7 in (48 cm) high. Lower end of a cross shaft fractured at the top. Background of plain shaft in key-pattern and spiral-work.

27.29: ✣ C.III. 1½ ft (46 cm) high. Fragment showing two priests or bishops with a crozier between them. Both wear vestments with embroidered hems. The figure on the right wears a pleated cope or cloak fastened at each shoulder with two round clasps or brooches. (*See* Invergowrie Panel in **NMS.**)

27.30: ✣ Fragment of sandstone *c.* 1 ft (30 cm) sculpted with spiral scroll and serpent's head.

Recent additions

A1: ✣ two robed priests with books.
A2: ✣ a small equal-armed cross with interlaced margin which may be part of recumbent stone.
A3: ✣ arm of a cross with a panel of decorated background.
A4: ✣ a plaster cast of the cup-marked base of 27.1.

28 Moonshade ✣ It was recorded in 1793 that two stand-ing stones were found near Cargill at NO 162 358. They are thought to have been buried soon after. One of these is said to have depicted moon and stars. Lost.

29 Murthly ✣ C.III. ORS. 3¾ ft (114 cm) long. This was found by the plough on the left bank of Gellyburn river close to where it flows into the Tay. **NMS** IB 101.
Front: an extraordinary panel reading left to right shows two men, one in a bird mask and the other in a dog mask fighting each other with swords and bossed shields. A pair of seahorses face each other with crossed forelegs while a naked man looks over his shoulder at a fanged bear-like beast of prey (maybe a manticora) which leaps towards him over a reptile resembling a crocodile with bug-eyes and a fish-tail.

30 New Scone ✛ 9/10th-century cross-slab. Yellowish grey sandstone. Identified in 1978 in a garden at NO 138 263. It was previously owned by a Perth family who gave it to their housekeeper on her retiral to Scone. It may have originally come from St John's kirkyard in Perth and before that from St Andrews. Now in **Perth Museum**.

Front and back: show almost identical round-armpit crosses with panels of key-pattern on either side of the shafts. The top of the crosses are broken off.

31 Pittensorn Farm ✛ C.III. Fragment found by the owner at the west of the farmhouse in 1994 near Gellyburn. NO 086 391. It may be the top left corner of a rectangular slab. **Perth Museum**.

Front: within the border moulding find two men grasping each other's wrists as if fighting over a ?book held by the figure on the right. Their legs are interlaced to the bottom of the panel. On the right of the men, are the hind parts of two beasts, one with a spiral tail.

32 Priest's Stone or **Chapel Stone** or **the Falls of Tummel** C.III. Mica schist. 4 ft (122 cm) high. Cross-slab which once stood on the west bank of the Tummel 2 miles (3.2 km) north-west of Pitlochry station at the edge of the water until the river was flooded to form the reservoir at Loch Faskally and the badly-weathered stone was moved up from the bank to NN 915 593.

One side: a worn cross.

Other side: traces of a warrior at the foot of the cross shaft.

33 Rossie Priory ✛ C.II. ORS. 5½ ft (168 cm) tall. Cross-slab found in old burial ground half a mile (0.8 km) east of Rossie Priory at NO 292 308. Now safely housed in the private chapel.

Front: a wonderfully decorated ringed and equal-armed cross on a shaft that stands well proud of the slab. The background is divided into four panels. Above left (1) a creature with a human face and beast's body, maybe a centaur. Above right (2) a bird-like creature attacked by a human in a bird-mask. Left background of the shaft and arranged vertically find (3) a beast with a tail curved over its back above a man seized by a fantastic beast above a pair of beasts facing each other. Right of the shaft (4) a beast interlaced with a serpent and biting its head above a beast with bug-eyes (like Gask). Below, a pair of interlaced creatures with human faces look in opposite directions.

Back: surrounded on three sides by a border of interlace, find an equal-armed cross with outline shaft. The three upper arms and central medallion are filled with superb interlace. Lower arm displays an important horseman, the main figure in the design – perhaps a king. Below him within the shaft find two more elite warriors on horseback. Left of the shaft, a crescent & V-rod set perpendicularly above a Pictish beast. At the bottom, a beast with knees doubled-up and head turned to face its serpent-ended tail. Right of the shaft find two hounds, a rider on a leaping horse and below another horse and rider. Above the left arm of the cross find a naked man clutching a pair of birds, thought to be cranes, by their necks. (The crane was deeply significant to Columba. He saw it as a harbinger from his home in Ireland – an exile like himself.) In the right corner is an angel.

Comment: This ranks with the finest cross-slabs for its superb design, excellent execution and great variety of image.

34 St Madoes

34.1: ✣ C.II. ORS. 5 ft 9 in (175 cm) tall. Cross-slab which used to stand in St Madoes churchyard at NO 196 213. In 1853, it was erected on a pedestal near the parish church. It was hidden within a wooden box without access until 1991. After conservation, it was erected at the far end of the entrance hall in **Perth Museum.** Unfortunately the back is reflected by a mirror and is almost impossible to see.

Front: two beasts with heads missing surmount stone. A ringed cross divided into 11 panels of varying inter-lace. The central square contains 12 spiralled bosses which surround a larger central boss (which might symbolise Christ surrounded by his 12 apostles). The background above the side arms show two fantastic beasts, heads turned to bite their bodies. The shaft backgrounds each shows two beasts with spiralled tails curled between their hind legs, following each other.

Back: divided into six panels reading from top; (1), (2) and (3) show three monks facing left with cowls raised, riding elongated horses. Harness-rings, bridles and straps are well detailed; (3) seems to be carrying a book satchel; (4) a double-disc & Z-rod on the right while (5) on the left a crescent & V-rod. Below in (6) a Pictish beast.

34.2: C.III. Sandstone. Upper part of ringed cross-slab, originally built into a wall of the Session House adjoining the church and removed to the kirkyard in 1881. Sculpted on all four sides and split down the middle.

Front: ornament defaced except for two triquetras, one in each top corner.

Back: defaced except for triquetra in the right corner.

Both edges: contain four-cord plait-work.

35 Strowan or Struan

35.1: C.I. Blue schistose slate. 4 ft 4 in (132 cm) tall. Broken away at the bottom. Find the slab in a newly-restored church on the south bank of the River Garry at NN 809 653.

PS: a double-disc & Z-rod next to part of an unidentified symbol.

35.2 & 35.3: These two rude cross-slabs of quartzose slate both *c.* 3½ ft (107 cm) high are also found in the churchyard.

No.1: a small incised cross on both sides.

No.2: a cross with rounded ends to the arms on one face.

Pictish sites without stones

36 Dundurn, Perthshire. NM 707 232. (*See* text). Timber-laced fort thought to have been a principal stronghold and royal palace of the Picts of Fortriu. Artifacts found by the Alcocks included a leather shoe. The ruins of a medieval church stand below this important fortress at NN 702 236.

37 Moncrieffe Hill, Perthshire. NO 135 200. May have been the scene of the Battle of Monad Croib in AD 729.

38 Schiehallion, Perthshire. NN 714 548. Probably the strong-hold of the Caledonian Picts.

39 Scone, Perth. NO 114 265. Seat of the Scots kingdom of Scone in the 10th century.

Aṉgus

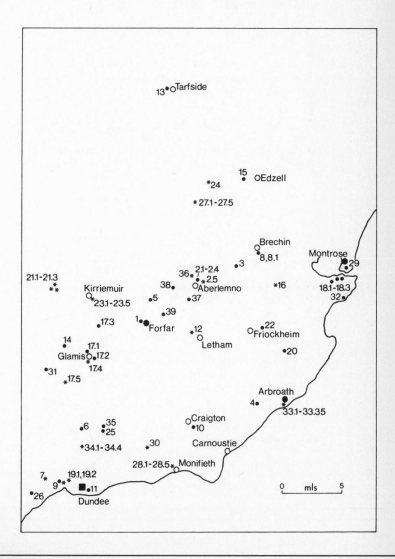

13 • ○Tarfside

15
• ○Edzell
*24

* 27.1-27.5

Brechin
○
8,8.1 • 3   Montrose
21.1-21.3   36 *2.1-2.4   • 29
 *   38 * • *2.5   *16   18.1-18.3
 * *   Kirriemuir   •   ○Aberlemno   • •
         ○   • 5 • 37   32 •
         * 23.1-23.5
                        • 39
              •17.3   1 •
                       •Forfar
         14   * 12   ○ • 22
         •   17.1   ○Letham   ○Friockheim
    Glamis○ •17.2
         * 17.4   • 20
 • 31   •17.5
         * 17.5
                                         Arbroath
                                        • 4 ●
                                          33.1-33.35
         • 6   •35   ○Craigton
              • 25   • 10
    * 34.1-34.4   * 30   Carnoustie
              28.1-28.5 * Monifieth   •
 7 *   19.1,19.2 ○
 9 • * * ■ • 11   0   mls   5
 • 26
    Dundee

1 The Meffan Institute, Forfar, known also as **Forfar Museum**, has recently (1995) added an extension mainly to display about 15 stones in need of a safe home. All these will be described in the text. The number includes two **EC** crosses and a Pillow Stone with a cross from Arbroath. It also houses the first new C.II stone to be found in Angus this century which was unearthed by the plough in April 1994 at Wester Denoon in Glamis Parish. Recently (1995) 17 further stones have been unearthed in the churchyard at Kirriemuir. They too will be displayed in the Meffan Institute. This small museum is a sophisticated Pictish Centre. Don't miss it!

Aberlemno village, well-named 'The Heart of Angus', is an oasis of peace lying between the South Esk and the Lunan rivers, protected by the twin hill-forts of Finavon and Turin. The parish has changed little over the years and still gives evidence of its huge importance not only in the Pictish era but also in prehistory. The beautiful Pitkennedy necklace of 100 beads was found nearby in a kist containing a female skeleton, while the Melgund necklace, found in 1980 in a low cist, points to a civilisation far older than the Picts. Later Malcolm II is said to have defeated the Danes in a battle fought here in 1012. The church first appears in written records dating to 1242, when it was dependant on Restenneth Priory and the Augustinian monks who owned it.

At present the famous Aberlemno stones are all boxed for protection from October to the end of April. Historic Scotland, however, is hoping to house them safely in a building near the church.

2 Aberlemno

2.1: C.I. 6 ft (183 cm) tall. Sandstone. This stands on the roadside ¼ mile (0.4 km) north of the church at NO 523 559 and is one of the finest of all C.I stones.
PS: a snake, double-disc & Z-rod with a mirror and comb below.

2.2: Aberlemno Kirkyard C.II. Yellowish **ORS.** 7½ ft tall. A pedimented ringed cross-slab – perhaps the finest in its class – stands in the kirkyard at NO 522 556.
Front: the quadrilobate cross, carved 3½ in (9 cm) proud of its background, is decorated with a wonderful selection of interlace. The central medallion contains seven triple spirals with S-shaped connections. (If the spiral symbolises God as the

centre of the universe round which all life revolves, then these are well-placed.)

Above the top arms find two worn fantastic beasts, while on either side of the shaft, the panels are filled with zoomorphic designs of the highest quality. Note the two graceful seahorses in the bottom right corner; above their fish-tails the small triquetra may represent the unity of the Trinity. It is thought that all the interlace here (and on all cross-slabs) is symbolic of a Christian theme and must have been carefully selected for the message as much as for the art.

Back: is framed by two open-jawed serpents whose heads meet in the apex of the pediment. They may or may not have a head between their jaws as on Dunfallandy. Below are two Pictish symbols, the notched rectangle & Z-rod and the cauldron. Below these, a battle scene, shown in cartoon fashion – a unique device in Pictish sculpture – seems to tell a story as follows: Row (1), a mounted Pictish warrior gives chase to a Northumbrian horseman with helmet and nose-guard who has thrown away his sword and shield. Both horses have undocked tails which may point to the importance of their riders. Row (2), three unhelmeted Pictish foot-soldiers in battle order about to attack a mounted Northumbrian warrior with nose-guard and raised spear. His horse's tail is docked. Row (3), a pair of warriors charge each other, one of whom – probably the Northumbrian – is helmeted with a nose-guard. The third man lies dead, food for the raven pecking his face. Note his long divided tunic possibly mail, his discarded shield and spear. The scene is thought to represent the **Battle of Nechtansmere (or Dunnichen)** fought in AD 685, during which King Brude mac Bili or his warriors killed the Anglian King Ecgfrid. Although the slab is thought to date to *c.* 750, the battle would be well-remembered in the oral tradition. A splendid cast made by **NMS** is on loan to the Meffan Institute, but the stone is in the care of HS.

2.3: C.II. Over 9 ft (274 cm) high. Badly weathered cross-slab situated on the roadside and sometimes called **The Mourning Angels** represents the Crucifixion and is full of emotion.

Front: the ringed cross stands on a lengthy shaft covered with interlace. The background has ten panels. The two above the arms of the cross seem to show beasts, the two below the arms have zoomorphic interlace. The two on either side of the top shaft show angels carved in deep relief, their heads bowed in adoration and grief. Below, find key patterning and on either side of the foot of the shaft some fantastic beasts.

Back: divided into three panels as follows: (1) ornamented crescent & V-rod above a double disc & Z-rod; (2) a hunting scene with four mounted men, three of them huntsmen with long horns (compare with Hilton of Cadboll). Another man faces the hunters, and there are three stags and three hounds; (3) divided into two panels, the left of which shows Chiron the centaur with a bird-like creature under his legs. The right shows King David as shepherd and psalmist rending the jaws of the lion, with sheep and harp.

Edges: both decorated with incised spirals.

2.4: C.I. This stands on the roadside between 2.1 and 2.3 at NO 522 558.
PS: traces of a crescent and a curved line.

2.5: Flemington Farm ✤ C.I. This was found by the plough in 1961 at NO 524 556. **Dundee Museum.**
PS: A Pictish beast and arch symbol.

3 Aldbar C.III. ORS. Cross-slab in Brechin Cathedral. It once stood in the mortuary chapel, built on the site of an ancient church at the foot of a wooded glen near Aldbar Castle at NO 573 582.

Front: a ringed cross decorated with six-cord plait terminating at the foot in a hollow rectangle, the sides of which are key-patterned. Left and right of top arm, two very worn birds may represent the cock that warned St Peter and the Holy Dove. Either side of the shaft are two seated monks with books and dressed in two styles of vestments which have interesting hollows in the centre of the hems. (Dr Bryce suggests that the cross is the Tree of Life standing on a square earth with the symbolic birds caught in its branches, or the journey all must make from this world to the next.)

Back: four distinct images may represent the Christian order of life. Two enthroned monks at the top might stand for the Church. David rending the lion's jaw, with harp, staff and sheep, might represent the kingdom while the mounted warrior symbolises subjects and the many-legged beast at the bottom, the animal world.

4 Arbirlot C.III Whinstone. 5½ ft (168 cm) high. This was found in the foundations of an old church *c.* 1836 and preserved in the manse garden. NO 601 404.
Front: two small crosses, one at the top and the other at the bottom with two rectangular figures like open books. The upper book has a small circle on the left and a zig-zag line connecting it to the lower cross. The lower book has a prong projecting from its left edge.

5 Baggerton ✢ C.I. Fragment in Rescobie parish, once said to been found in area of Baggerton farm at NO *c.* 469 537. It may have had a snake and a sceptre incised on it. Presumably lost.

6 Balludernon or **St Martin's Stone C.II.** Sandstone. 4 ft (122 cm) high. Cross-slab with the top broken away. In a field south of South Balluderon farmhouse, west of the A929 at NO 3748 3758.
Front: part of a horseman in the lower shaft of the cross.
PS: a Pictish beast left of a horseman above a snake & Z-rod.
Front: an ornate cross with an angel in each panel above the arms. Lower left panel, two twisted creatures facing each other. Right panel displays two intertwined serpents with protruding tongues, back to back.
Back: two mounted, armed warriors, one above the other, in full battle gear wearing helmets with long nose guards similar to the Anglian warriors of Aberlemno Churchyard. A dog can be seen between the hooves of the upper horse.

7 Benvie Churchyard ✢ late **C.III.** Cross-slab originally found 2 miles (3.2 km) north-west of Invergowrie on a minor road at NO 328 314. A cast has been placed in the local churchyard while the original stone, beautifully conserved, is in **Dundee Museum**.

8 Brechin Cathedral, noted for its Irish-style Round Tower dating to the 11th century, houses five sculptured stones one of which is a mere fragment of a cross-slab. Two are Hogback gravestones *c.*11th century. One is Aldbar. The other is described below.

OPEN: 5-9 pm daily in summer and in winter on Monday, Tuesday, Thursday, Friday from 2-4 pm and on Sundays when open for worship.

8.1: Brechin Cathedral (Virgin and Child) **C.III** or 11th century. Dug up in a garden which had once been part of an ancient churchyard. It was put in the old chapel of Aldbar then returned to the Cathedral and fixed to the north wall of the chancel.

Front: Latin cross with a large circular medallion surrounded by pelleted or jewelled frame. This contains the Virgin with a very large Child above an inscription which reads in angular Hiberno-Saxon minuscules S MARIA MR CHR (St Mary, Mother of Christ). She wears a wide hat similar to Monifieth 29.2. In the top right arm, a bird may represent the Holy Dove with the Man symbol of St Matthew above the left arm and the Calf of St Luke to the right. Two angels in the side arms support the central medallion, while the Eagle of St John and the Lion of St Mark may be seen either side of the lower shaft. Within the lower shaft are the heads of two saints with haloes, one of whom seems to be St Peter with key.

Edges: in the panels corresponding to the arms of the cross find two human figures.

9 Bullion, Invergowrie ✤. **C.III.** Found at NO 343 305. This shows an old warrior with shield awry, balding head, untrimmed beard, bulbous nose and pot-belly riding an equally jaded horse. The old warrior drinks from a horn with the terminal showing a bird's head with an amused yet scornful expression. **NMS** IB 229.

10 Camus Cross ✤ **C.III. ORS.** Badly worn free-standing cross in private grounds at Panmure House, Craigton. NO 519 379.

Front: three panels as follows; (1) crucifixion with sponge- and spear-bearers on either side of the arms; (2) Sagittarius and (3) scrolls of foliage in shaft.

Back: three panels containing (1) Christ in the act of benediction with his right hand and a book in his left hand. A seraph kneels in the left arm and an archangel in the right; (2) and (3) the four haloed

Evangelists holding their Gospel books.

Edges: carved in patterns of interlaced foliage.

Comment: This unusual stone, one of the few to portray the Crucifixion, should be conserved and placed in a church visible to all and safe from further weathering.

Dundee Museum and Art Gallery

11 Dundee Museum at the McManus Galleries, Albert Square, Dundee, houses the story of life in Tayside from prehistoric times to the present day, and includes an excellent section on the Picts with five stones at present in its permanent collection.

OPEN: every day except Sundays from 10am-5pm.

12 Dunnichen stone ✤ **C.I.** Sandstone. Under 5 ft (152 cm). This is said to have been found in 1811 in a field belonging to East Mains of Dunnichen farm on the edge of or inside the marsh identified as Nechtansmere. Allegedly a stone coffin containing bones lay beneath it. It was first removed to the church in Dunnichen and then taken to Dunnichen House before being housed in **Dundee Museum.** An excellent cast has been erected on its previous site at NO *c.* 516 496. At the time of writing, the original cast is about to be moved to the **Meffan Institute, Forfar.**

PS: beautifully incised with the flower above a double-disc & Z-rod with a mirror and comb below.

Comment: Dunnichen Hill may have been site of the Battle of Nechtansmere in AD 685. Many gather here every May to celebrate the victory of the Picts over the Anglians. Some who go for the sake of a party never realise that if the Picts had not won this battle Scotland might never have existed. A sobering thought.

13 Drostan's Stone, Tarfside, Glenesk. **EC** cross incised on a boulder lying south of the track that leads west from St Drostan's Episcopal Church. Many sites in this remote area are associated with this missionary monk. Reach it by taking the side road a mile north of Edzell that follows the glen up the east side of the River North Esk at NO 484 798.

14 Eassie C.II. Cross-slab which stands within the ruins of Eassie Church at NO 353 474. It was recently housed by Historic Scotland within the church in a glass case.

Front: a finely decorated equal-armed cross on a long shaft with connecting ring. The background above the top arms shows two cherubim. Left of the shaft, an armed warrior strides purposefully toward the right, while in the right lower panel find a stag above a beast with its tail between its legs. Below, a running hound. *Back:* divided into two panels; (1) top left shows a Pictish beast above a double-disc & Z-rod. Below left, three robed figures in procession carry poles. To the right find a tub with an apple tree next to a man with a rod over his shoulder, perhaps Adam as gardener with the Tree of Life; panel (2) (lower) is badly worn but parts of two or three cows with spiral curves and what may be an arch are just visible. Because of the shallow delicacy of the carving, Eassie may be one of the earliest cross-slabs dating from around AD 750.

15 Edzell Castle, in the care of Historic Scotland, is open in summer from 9.30 am-6 pm on weekdays and 2-6 pm on Sundays. From October-March it closes at 4 pm.

The 9th-century **C.III** fragment of a free-standing decorated cross was found in the old kirkyard nearby at NO 583 687. It is now displayed in a summer-house at Edzell.

16 Farnell ✣ **C.III. ORS.** 6¾ ft (206 cm) tall with pediment. Cross-slab found in Farnell kirkyard in 1849 at NO 627 554. **Montrose Museum**.

Front: the interlaced and ringed cross is very worn. The background is divided into six panels filled with zoomorphic interlace, diagonal key-pattern and four-cord plaiting.

Back: surrounded by pelleted margin, erased in many places, and forming the bodies of two fanged serpents which confront each other in the apex of the pediment (*see* Dunfallandy). Below find the head and part of the right wing of the large angel who guarded the entrance to Eden. Lower middle shows a small ringed-cross, perhaps representing salvation through the Cross of Christ. Below, Adam and Eve clothed, stand either side of an apple tree. Eve on the right holds an apple while two serpents fill the vacant spaces either side of them, possibly to give symmetry to the design. These images seem to represent the Fall and Rise of Man.

17 Glamis Manse

17.1: C.I and **C.II. ORS.** 8¼ ft (251 cm) high by 5½ ft (168 cm) wide. Ringed cross-slab which stands in the manse garden at the east end of Glamis village at NO 386 469. This magnificent stone, with its incised symbols on the back and relief cross and carvings on the front, combines both C.I and C.II motifs on the same stone.

Front: a cross with pedimented top divided into five interlaced panels, including a central circular inter-laced medallion. The background contains four subjects as follows: top left, a lion-like beast with a tail curved over its back (perhaps symbolising St Mark). Top right, a centaur with an axe in each hand, is Chiron, who chopped down the healing branch of the centaury plant and gave it to Aesculapius, Greek god of medicine (may symbolise Christ the Healer). Lower left, a cauldron with human legs protruding from it above two warriors in short tunics fighting with axes. (The cauldron may represent the Celtic Cauldron of Regeneration capable of healing battle wounds.) Lower right, a beast's head above a cauldron.

Back: C.I incised symbols of snake, salmon and mirror.

Comment: Though designs on Pictish stones are mostly eclectic, the various themes here might draw together to symbolise holy healing. **St Fergus Well**, still used for baptisms, can be seen by the river.

17.2: C.I and **C.II.** 5 ft (152 cm) high. Cross-slab which stands in a wood on the north slope of Hunter's Hill about half a mile (0.4 km) south-east of Glamis church at NO 394 465. Take the track opposite the exit from Glamis village south of the A94.

Front: an equal-armed cross on a shaft within a defaced plaited border. Background is divided into four panels as follows: (1) above the top left arm, a cherub with four wings similar to Eassie; (2) above the right arm, a bird-headed man carries an axe and confronts part of another figure; (3) left of the shaft some deer. Right of the shaft, two beasts with tails curled between their legs above (4) cauldron and flower symbols.

Back: incised beast and snake, and part of a mirror.

17.3: St Orland's Stone, Cossans. **C.II.** *c.* 7¾ ft (236 cm) high. Cross-slab once surrounded by marsh which may have been covered with water for many centuries. It probably marked the site of an ancient chapel. NO 401 500.

Front: a full length ringed-cross with spirals interlace and highly ornate zoomorphic patterns.

Back: framed by two serpents whose fish tails appear at the centre foot of the stone and jaws at the centre top. The jaws appear to be holding something which might – as on Dunfallandy – be a human head. From the top of the stone find a crescent & V-Rod, double-disc & Z-Rod, a recess where the stone is cracked, two horsemen in single file, another two horsemen followed by two hounds, a boat containing several figures. The large object at the right end of the boat may be cargo or possibly Christ with his four evangelists. Below, a beast attacking a bull or cow.

17.4 Glamis: ✣ C.I. Irregular fragment showing a diamond-shaped ?symbol with a spiral in the centre linked to a broken-off portion of what might be a similar shape. **Meffan Institute, Forfar**.

17.5 Wester Denoon: ✣ C.II. *c.* 850. Damaged centre of a cross-slab found by the plough near Glamis in 1994. NO 350 433. **Meffan Institute, Forfar**.

Front: an interlaced Latin cross infilled with thick knotwork. The background shows linked rectangles filled with crosses.

Back: dominated by a human figure, the top of whose head is missing. Thought to be a woman, she faces forward and wears a gown with a decorated hem and diagonal stripes across the breast, fastened at the shoulders. She wears a huge penannular brooch (compare with the ?brooch on **Hilton of Cadboll** woman). The figure is seen as a woman because of the distinctive mirror and comb symbols on the left. On the right, a panel of interlace.

18 Inchbrayock

18.1 Samson Stone: ✣ C.III. ORS. 2½ ft tall (76 cm) 9th-10th century. Delightful small cross-slab found in 1849 in the old kirkyard at St. Brioch on the south side of Rossie Island, just south of Montrose in the middle of the River South Esk. NO 710 567. **Montrose Museum**.

Front: a decorated ringed cross with stepped armpits, a spiral pattern in the arms and key pattern in the centre. The upper background displays zoomorphic interlace. In the left lower background, a rampant or possibly prone beast with a reptile between its hind and front legs. It is thought to represent the lion slain by Samson from which 'came forth sweetness'. In the right panel, a beast-headed Delilah cutting off the sleeping Samson's hair. You can clearly see the shears in her hand.

Back: the top shows an armed and mounted warrior surrounded by strange creatures, one of which may be a hound leaping towards that familiar beast with legs tucked under its body. The same creature appears in the right corner above the warrior's head. The Tree of Life (perhaps) is carved in the form of the tempting serpent with the fruit as ornamented discs. This upper scene perhaps symbolises Samson as warrior-hunter on his journey through life. Below, Samson with his long hair in the centre slaying the Philistine with the jaw-bone of an ass. Note the jaw-bone is incorrectly devised. Behind him perhaps a dead Philistine prone with knees drawn up and eyes closed. Others link this figure to Samson's mother miraculously pregnant. Unlikely, I think.

18 2: C.III. ORS. Upper part of a cross-slab discovered in 1857 on the same site as 18.1.
Front: two eagle-winged and headed men facing left.
Back: a warrior on a cantering horse.

18 3: is the middle part of a slab said to be in Craig Manse NO 704 562. A hunting scene.

19 Invergowrie ✣ These stones were noticed built one above the other into a window opening of the old ruined church of St Peter (NO 350 303) before being removed to **NMS** IB 251 and 257.
19.1: ✣ **C.III. ORS.** Cross-slab 2¾ ft high (84 cm).
Front: an exquisitely ornamented ringed cross. The background shows four panels filled with assorted interlace.
Back: three monks are allegedly St Curadan/Boniface with two companions sent by Abbot Ceolfrid from Northumberland at the request of King Nechtan mac Derile to instruct Pictish church in Roman usages c.710. They may have landed at Gowrie on the Tay. The centre monk holds a book and the handle of a purse-like object which may be a reliquary or ?musical instrument. The other two hold books. The shoulder discs on the two companion monks contain

equal-armed crosses. Below, two intertwined beasts with fanged jaws bite each other's tails. A perfect gem of a cross-slab.

19.2: ✛ the middle part of a small, ornamented, badly-worn cross.
Front: left of the lower arm is the head of a beast, while on the right perhaps an L-shaped object.
Back: the lower parts of two men and an angel above the upper part of an armed warrior.

20 Kinblethmont House, Inverkeillor. ✛ **C.I.** This was found by the plough in 1952. It is preserved at Kinblethmont House at NO 638 473.
PS: a crescent & V-rod, Pictish beast and the top of a mirror and comb.

21 Kingoldrum church is 4 miles (6.4 km) west of Kirriemuir at NO 334 550. Three stones were found while pulling down the old kirk all of which are in **NMS** Edinburgh.
21.1: ✛ **C.II.** Cross-slab 2 ft (6l cm) high. **NMS** IB 39.
Front: a full-length cross with rectangular extensions to the arms and ornamented with key patterns. The background shows a pair of interlaced serpents.
Back: at the top, two enthroned figures with the one on the right much bigger than the other. Both heads are missing. Below left, mirror above crescent. Below right, step symbol with ?sheep above and double-sided comb below.
21.2: ✛ **C.III.** *c.* 3 ft (91 cm) tall. Most of a cross slab sculptured on one side only. **NMS** IB 40.
Front: a decorated cross with a triple spiral in the central circle.
21.3: ✛ **C.III** fragment.
Front: part of a Maltese cross.
Back: part of a Crucifixion scene with a very crude figure of Christ. **NMS** IB 41l.

22 Kinnell C.II. Whinstone. This forms part of the coping on the north wall of the manse garden about 2 miles (3.2 km) east of Friockham. NO 609 502.
Front edge: two incised, coiled and adjacent serpents looking away from each other.

23 Kirriemuir Five stones were found here in 1787 when

Collessie, Fife, an ancient standing stone re-used by the Picts? (Photo: T. E. Gray)

Fowlis Wester Church, Perthshire. (Photo: T. E. Gray)

Rossie Priory.
(Photo: T. E. Gray, courtesy Lord Kinnaird)

Meigle Museum No 5, Perthshire.

(Photo: T. E. Gray, courtesy Historic Scotland)

Aberlemno No 3, Angus.

(Photo: T. E. Gray)

Wester Denoon,
Meffan Institute,
Forfar.

(Photo: T. E. Gray,
courtesy Angus
Museums)

Inchbrayock,
Angus.

(Photo: T. E. Gray,
courtesy Angus
Museums)

Farnell,
Montrose
Museum.

(Photo: T. E. Gray,
courtesy Angus
Museums)

The Maiden
Stone, near
Inverurie.

(Photo: T. E. Gray)

Migvie, near Tarland, Kincardine and Deeside.
(Photo: T. E. Gray)

One of a pair of stones at Congash, near Grantown, which appear to act as 'gateposts' to an ancient circular religious site.

(Photo: T. E. Gray)

Rosemarkie Stone, Ross and Cromarty, the pride of Groam House Pictish Museum, Rosemarkie.

(Photo: T. E. Gray, courtesy Groam House Museum)

Hilton of Cadboll.

(Photo: T. E. Gray courtesy NMS)

Edderton, Ross and Cromarty. Possibly a Bronze Age standing stone, re-used by the Picts to carve double disc and Z-rod with salmon.

(Photo: T. E. Gray)

The Ulbster stone, Caithness, now in Thurso Museum.
(Photo: T. E. Gray, courtesy Thurso Museum)

Golspie No 2, Sutherland, now in Dunrobin Museum.

(Photo: T. E. Gray, courtesy Lord Strathnaver)

The Mail
Stone,
Shetland
Museum.
(Photo: Shetland
Museum)

Raasay.
(Photo: T.E. Gray)

Tote, Isle of Skye.
(Photo: T. E. Gray)

the old Church of St Mary was demolished. They were placed in the graveyard at NO 386 539. Recently removed for conservation, they are now all on display at the **Meffan Institute, Forfar**. In 1995, 17 further fragments were excavated prior to the enlargement of the entrance to Kirriemuir Parish Church. These included one complete, though broken, cross-slab similar to Kirriemuir 23.5. All of the fragments were found in the base of a wall which Norman Atkinson, Angus District Curator, thinks might have been part of the pre-1787 churchyard. All but one were used as building material and may have been deliberately broken. This hoard indicates the importance of Kirriemuir as a Pictish ecclesiastical site comparable to Meigle. All are housed in the **Meffan Institute**.

23.1: ✣ C.II. ORS. Small cross-slab.
Front: a Latin cross filled with interlace. The two top background panels would seem to contain two ecclesiastics in profile, one with a bird-mask, the other's head is missing. The two lower figures facing forward are ecclesiastics with books. (Possibly the four figures represent Saints Matthew, Luke, Mark and John).
Back: two panels; (1) two monks bow to each other, both holding between them a circular object. These may be Saints Paul and Anthony breaking the loaf in the wilderness. A third figure – a cloaked ecclesiastic or possibly an angel – stands to the right; (2) shows an enthroned figure, possibly a woman, with a mirror & comb to the left. An unrecognisable object, thought by some to be a stringed instrument or loom on the right.

23.2: ✣ C.II. ORS. Small cross-slab.
Front: decorated cross on a shaft with part of the pedestal. Bottom panel in the shaft, two beasts with paws in each other's mouth. Background of the shaft is divided into four panels; (1) two angels kneel in adoration; (2) left of the shaft, a striding bearded man with long hair curled at the ends wears what looks like a kilt and plaid drawn over his shoulders. He holds a staff in his left hand; (3) right of the shaft, a bird of prey with a beak fixed in the back of a dying stag; (4) below, two animals and a hound.
Back: an elaborate hunting scene. Left of the top, find a double-disc & Z-rod. The upper mounted warrior holds his large horse on a tight rein so that its bowed head can fit within the recessed frame. The rider

below at full gallop with raised weapon is about to strike a stag being bitten in its hindquarters by a leaping hound under the horse's belly.

23.3: ✦ C.III. ORS. Lower half of a cross-slab.
Front: shaft and parts of the lower arms filled with six-cord plait, while the background panels are filled with zoomorphic plaiting.
Back: the top shows part of the legs and jaws of a horse which probably had a rider. Below, a mounted warrior with a pronounced eye shaped like a key-hole (similar to Benvie). His short body fits the confined space. To the left, a small hound and to the right, interlace ending in a triquetra.
Left side: plaited interlace.

23.4: ✦ C.III. ORS. Lower 2 ft (61 cm) of a cross-slab. Back and left side broken away.
Front: right edge is bordered with a key pattern. Centre is filled with a remarkably elaborate, bare-footed angel, whose robe is exquisitely decorated and edged in key-pattern and whose delightful wings are similar to those on the Benvie stone.
Right edge: part of three-cord plait-work, double-beaded.

23.5: ✦ C.III. Small near-rectangular cross-slab with undecorated crosses on both sides and knot-work in the background. Front is bordered with square key-work.

24 Lethnott ✦ C.III. 9 in (23 cm) high. Fragment found in 1884 while repairing the floor of a church. Lethnott is 7 miles (11 km) north-west of Brechin beyond the Brown and White Caterthun. **NMS** IB 132.
Front: part of a small cross with spirals and interlace.
Back: Latin inscription in Hiberno-Saxon capitals with a few minuscules which reads 'Son of Medicius'.

25 Linlathen ✦ C.I. Fragment said to have been found in Cairn Greig NO 466 338 in 1834 and removed to Linlathen House in 1864 at NO 463 329. Lost.
PS: most of a Pictish beast.

26 Longforgan C.I. Fragment found during agricultural operations in 1966 at NO 306 299. This stood in a churchyard until recently when a fly-over was proposed. Historic Scotland, while checking for vulnerable sites,

was given the stone by the local minister for safe-keeping. Its ultimate destination is not yet known.
PS: roughly incised double-dis*c*.

27 Menmuir

27.1: ✤ **C.III. ORS.** *c.* 3½ ft (107 cm) high. Very worn cross-slab discovered leaning against the north wall at Menmuir Church some 9 miles (14.5 km) south-west of Edzell at NO 534 643. **Meffan Institute, Forfar**.
Front: head of the cross has an irregular key-pattern while most of the sculpture on the shaft is defaced. The foot contains some irregular interlace. The figure of an ecclesiastic to the right of the shaft.
Back: a coiled fish creature with a large eye above a mounted warrior with a sea-beast above his right shoulder. Below, another mounted warrior with a man brandishing a club-like object behind him.

27.2: ✤
Front: **C.III** or **EC** grave marker with tenon to fit into recumbent stone. *c.* 1 ft (30 cm) high. A man on horseback surrounded by a border of very worn key-pattern.
Back: the lower part of an ecclesiastic. **Meffan Institute**.

27.3: ✤ **C.III.** Fragment of a hunting scene showing parts of two mounted and armed warriors above a hound attacking a stag. **Meffan Institute**.

27.4: ✤ **C.III.** Top part of a small rounded cross-slab, showing a very worn decorated cross against a plain background. The upper edges of the arms are curved like wings. **Meffan Institute**.

27.5: ✤ **EC.** Deeply incised cross on a plain background. **Meffan Institute**.

28 Monifieth ✤

Five stones were found in the foundations of the old parish church and built into the wall of a new church in 1812 at NO 495 324 before being acquired by **NMS** before 1903.

28.1: C.II. ORS. Small cross-slab.
Front: a cross extends full length of the stone. Decorated with three types of key pattern. The background is recessed but not decorated.
Back: a double-disc at the top above a comb. To the

left: double-disc & Z-rod to the right set perpendicularly above upper rim of a mirror. **NMS** IB 26.

28.2: ✤ **C.II.** 1½ ft (46 cm) high by 1 ft (30 cm) wide. Small cross-slab decorated on both sides and more or less complete.

Front: a cross with five panels including a central square filled with triangular interlace. The other panels are filled with spirals and interlace.

Back: the top panel shows a pair of beaked monsters facing each other with claws upraised above a creature with reptilian head to the left and the beast's head symbol to the right. The left bottom panel shows a woman (possibly) facing the front wearing a large hat and long cloak. Some say she wears a penannular brooch. The hat resembles the Virgin's head-dress on the Brechin stone. In the right panel find a double-disc & Z-rod set perpendicularly. **NMS** IB 27.

28. 3: ✤ **C.II. ORS.** Fragment showing top section of cross shaft. Badly defaced.

Front: the decoration is too hard to make out. Left of the shaft, a beast with four legs above a long-necked bird seizing the back of a man's neck. Their bodies may be interlaced. Right of the shaft, some beasts.

Back: may show a horseman, long-necked bird, beast with its tail between its legs, stag and hound and (as on Dunfallandy) a pair of monsters holding a human head between their open jaws. **NMS** IB 28.

28.4: ✤ **C.III. ORS.** c. 4 ft (122 cm) tall. Shaft of free-standing cross skilfully sculpted and carved on all four sides.

Front: divided into four panels as follows: (1) the tunic and legs of a crucified Christ with possibly Saints John and Mary on each side; (2) two monks holding horns; (3) an accurate portrayal of man playing harp.

Back: interlace with a beast biting its own neck at the bottom.

Right side: interlace and crouched creature with its tail between its legs.

Left side: interlace with a beast with reptilian head looking over its shoulder. **NMS** IB 25.

28.5: ✤ part of cross-slab. **NMS** IB 210.

29 Montrose Museum, Panmure Place, is one of the most visitor-friendly small museums in Scotland. Its

Pictish display offers plenty of activities for children (of all ages) to enjoy. The several stones on display include two from Inchbrayock and the Farnell 'Adam and Eve' cross-slab which should not be missed.
OPEN: Monday – Saturday 10am – 5pm.

30 Murroes ✤ C.III. Fragment of a cross-slab found when levelling a churchyard in 1896, NO 461 351. **NMS** IB 166.
Front: the lower portion of the shaft of a decorated cross with a creature rampant in right background.

31 Nevay EC. Circular stone with deeply incised cross from Nevay Church (Kirkinch) NO 332 449, found in 1988 by N.M. Robertson. **Meffan Institute**.

32 St Skae EC. Two incised crosses on the wall of the ruined church 2 miles (3.2 km) south of Montrose on an imposing cliff-top. NO 715 540.

33 St Vigeans Museum, Arbroath The Royal Burgh of Arbroath is famous for its Tironensian Abbey. Founded by William I in 1178 and dedicated to St Thomas Becket, it dominates the town. Less flamboyant, but of intense historical interest, St Vigeans Museum, tucked into a valley barely two miles (3.2 km) north of Arbroath, is equally the treasure-house of an earlier Celtic missionary monk from Ireland who died in AD 664. His foundation is such an important Christian site that every Pictophile should see it at NO 638 429.

The museum's collection is housed in a cottage converted in 1961 by Historic Scotland in a quiet lane close to the church. Inside you will be overwhelmed by the sight of 35 (less three that are lost) carved stones and fragments ranging in date from the 8th to the 10th centuries. Note the amount of tiny fragments which suggests that there must have been a period of hideous destruction in the lives of these precious relics.

33.1 ✤ C.II. ORS. 6 ft (183 cm) tall. Cross-slab found in two pieces during the restoration of a church in 1872. Cemented together, it is now the centre-piece of the museum.
Front: the cross extends the full length of the stone and is filled with double-beaded interlace. Left background above the arms is an impish winged creature which might be a 'sheila-na-gig' or fertility symbol more usually seen in Irish or English country churches.

Left background of the shaft, from the top, shows a reptile and serpent, and two interlaced serpents with winged dragon below. Right background, a beast with four legs and a swan-like neck, a four-legged beast with claws and bared teeth, and at the bottom another beast with a swan neck and bristled back above two interlaced serpents.

Front: from the top, a hunting scene with two hounds chasing a stag, a small creature and portions of others below. A double-disc & Z-rod above a crescent with a mirror & comb to its right. Below, a group of animals, including a large beast (?bear), a hind suckling its young, a creature with its tail between its legs, a large beast with a single curved horn, an eagle grabbing a fish in its talons (perhaps symbolising Christ as the eagle rescuing the human soul from the waters of sin). Finally an archer wearing a cloak with a peaked hood shooting at a boar with a cross-bow. (*See* Shandwick, Glenfurness and Meigle 10).

Right Edge: two panels; (1) filled with interlace while (2) contains a slab bearing an incised inscription in Hiberno-Saxon rounded minuscules which reads: *Drosten ipe Uoret ett Forcus.*

Left edge: scrolls of foliage.

33.2: ✤ **C.II. ORS.** 3 ft 8 in (112 cm) tall. Shaft of a cross-slab divided into three panels of interlace, diagonal key-pattern and spirals. Right background, part of a mirror or double-disc with a serpent & Z-Rod above an eagle.

33.3: ✤ **C.II.** Tiny part of a slab showing a portion of a double-disc & Z-rod.

33.4: ✤ **C.II. ORS.** Small part of a cross-slab showing the left corner of a ringed-cross with triquetra in the background.
Back: the upper part of a cowled monk facing left, with a staff or crozier behind him and a double-disc at the right edge.

33.5: ✤ **C.II. ORS.** Tiny fragment of a cross-slab showing a small portion of a decorated rectangular symbol with a double-disc & Z-Rod below.

33.6: ✤ **C.II.** Fragment of a cross-slab with interlace on the front and double-disc & Z-rod on the back. Each disc contains four raised bosses with spirals set against a background of trumpet-shaped expansions and vesica-shaped spots in the style of Celtic illuminated manuscripts.

33.7: ✤ C.III. ORS. 5 ft 6 in (168 cm) tall. Cross-slab which stood in the churchyard when first described in 1856. *Front:* a cross with seven decorated panels on a rectangular plinth. Note the single spirals that extend from each end of the round armpits. Left background of the shaft contains two important clerics in vestments and shoes, holding a third figure upside down over a square block or container. Below them two further monks with folded hoods on cloaks worn over elaborate priestly vestments carry staves and wear tongued shoes. This is a scene associated with ritual drowning or as Dr John Higgitt suggests the destruction in Rome of heretic, Simon Magus, by the prayers of the Saints Peter and Paul. The right background contains two seated monks sharing a circular loaf, almost certainly Saints Anthony and Paul with the crow's gift of bread in the wilderness. (*See* Nigg pediment). Below, an emaciated naked figure kneels before a bull with a stick or knife pointed at its throat. The starveling with out-thrust scrolled tongue may be about to sacrifice the bull. This may symbolise the Biblical theme that the blood of bulls and goats satisfies no-one in comparison with the saving blood of Christ, or he may simply be bleeding the beast for sustenance as was done in the pre-summer months in the Highlands as late as the 19th century. *Back:* apart from faint traces of a cross, the sculpture has been cruelly defaced.

33.8: ✤ C.III. ORS. 5½ ft (168 cm) long. Narrow recumbent block showing a frieze of beasts in five panels, one of which is empty. Reading from left to right, a stag and hind, a dog, a beast with lolling tongue, a missing panel and a bird with elaborate feathers, perhaps a phoenix or peacock.

33.9: ✤ Fragment of a free-standing cross which is still to be moved from a buttress of the church.

33.10: ✤ C.III. ORS. 2 ft (61 cm) tall. Cross-slab with a pediment at the top and a tenon for fitting into a socket at the bottom.
Front: a cross decorated with interlace and knotwork. Background, two graceful birds attached by their feet to the upper arm. Two panels of interlace on either side of the shaft.
Back: a crescent-shaped arch ornamented with four-

cord plait-work under which two enthroned figures are seated.

33.11: ✠ C.III. *c.* 3 ft (91 cm) tall. Arbroath pavement-stone. Cross-slab.

Front: a decorated ringed cross with spiralled ends on the arms and bold key-pattern at the foot of the shaft. Background on either side of lower arm and shaft, triquetra knots. Below, a monk with a book and an angel.

Back: a pair of enthroned clerics each holding a book and flabellum fan. Flabellums are still used by deacons in Eastern churches as fans, to keep flies and dust off sacred elements during Eucharist. Made of feathers or metal engraved with feathers, they symbolise wings of seraphim and cherubin. Below are two further monks wearing waist-length hooded garments and holding staves. The man on the right seems to be wearing short trousers or a knee-length tunic with a half-moon piece cut out of the hem.

33.12: ✠ C.III. ORS. 2½ ft (76 cm) tall. The lower part of a cross-slab in two pieces.

Front: a dear little decorated cross on an arched base. (?Calvary)

33.13: ✠ ORS. 3¼ ft (99 cm) long. Part of a recumbent slab which has been broken away at one end and one side.

Top: rectangular recessed panels in the centre containing (1) a beaded, ornamented and ringed cross and (2) a circular medallion and part of a second similar cross. The border round the recess is filled with zoomorphic plait-work.

33.14: ✠ ORS. Recumbent monument in two pieces, wider at the top (3½ ft/107 cm) than at the bottom (2 ft/61 cm); (1) shows at the head, a border of spirals next to a socket for the cross, and a border of interlace; (2) the border continues as before to the bottom edge which is decorated with spirals.

Side: an incised man seated between two beasts (Daniel?) and, at the left, the head of a man and a beast.

33.15: ✠ ORS. *c.* 1 ft (30 cm) square. Head of a free-standing ringed-cross with a quadruple spiral in the centre and a diagonal key-pattern in the arms.

33.16: ✠ ORS. 3¼ ft (38 cm) tall. Erect pillar cross-slab with a Latin cross on a rectangular base, decorated in key-pattern.

33.17: ✤ **ORS.** *c.* 1 ft (30 cm) square. Fragment of a cross-slab.
Front: the lower part of a ringed-cross with ecclesiastics holding books on either side of the shaft.
Back: a man on horseback.

33.18: ✤ **ORS.** 1 ft 2 in (36 cm) square. Fragment of a cross-slab.
Front: the middle of the shaft with a square key-work.
Back: the middle portion of an enthroned figure holding a book.

33.19: ✤ **ORS.** 1 ft (30 cm) tall. Left upper corner of a ringed cross-slab.
Front: a griffin between a ring and decorated top arm.
Back: a deer with its legs doubled beneath its body.

33.20: ✤ **ORS.** 1¼ft (38 cm) tall. Fragment showing a griffin.

33.21: ✤ **ORS.** Under 1 ft (30 cm). Fragment of a cross-slab.
Front: portion of the top and left arm of a ringed cross.
Back: the head of a horse and a single spiral.

33.22: ✤ **ORS.** Tiny lower part of a cross-slab, showing the bottom of the shaft on the front and a rider on the back.

33.23: ✤ **ORS.** Tiny middle part of a cross-slab, chipped all round edges, ornamented with a single key-pattern.

33.24: ✤ Fragment of the corner of a cross-slab.
Front: part of the top arm is carved in a key-pattern with a scroll of foliage to the right.
Back: part of the top arm is ornamented with interlace, with the upper part of a beast to the right.

33.25: ✤ **ORS.** Tiny fragment of cross-slab, showing a man hanging on to the neck of a horse.

33.26: ✤ **ORS.** Tiny triangular fragment of a cross arm ornamented with a diagonal key-pattern. Lost.

33.27: ✤ **ORS.** Tiny semi-circular fragment showing a spiral.

33.28: ✤ **ORS.** Triangular fragment with the head of a man. Lost.

33.29: ✤ **ORS.** 5 ft (152 cm) long. Hogback coped monument with scales like roofing tiles on the top.

33.30: ✤ Small stone with a plain cross.

33.31: ✤ Tiny worn upper part of a cross-slab, with crosses on both sides.

33.32: ✤ Small fragment of a cross-slab showing a central boss and one arm of a cross in low relief. Debased interlace.

33.33: ✤ Tiny fragment of **EC** stone. Design undetermined.

33.34: ✤ Small fragment of a very worn design.

33.35: ✤ Small fragment of red sandstone with traces of possible scale pattern.

34 The Strathmartine Stones, once numbered 13 or 14. 34.1 and 34.2 are in **Dundee Museum,** 34.4 is in **NMS Edinburgh** and the rest were lost before 1903. The majority came from the district in and about the old church of St Martin some 5 miles (8 km) north-west of Dundee at NO 378 354.

34.1: ✤ **C.I.** Whinstone. *c.* 3 ft (91 cm) high.
PS: a crescent & V-rod over a Pictish beast.

34.2: ✤ **C.III. ORS.** Part of a recumbent slab. Border decorated with spirals. The centre is filled with two serpents biting each other's necks.

34.4: ✤ **C.II.** Fragment of a cross-slab. **ORS** Decorated on two sides. **NMS** IB 47.
    Front: spiral and zoomorphic interlace.
    Back: perhaps part of a Pictish beast.

35 Tealing Church C.II. ORS. Fragment of a cross-slab originally built into the south wall some 6 miles (9.7 km) north-east of Strathmartine. Souterrain sites in the area suggest a significant Pictish community. NO 404 379.

36 Woodrae (Woodwray) ✤ **C.II. ORS.** 5¾ ft (175 cm) high. Cross-slab found while clearing the foundations of Woodwray Castle at NO 518 566. It was later taken to the garden at Abbotsford, home of Sir Walter Scott in the Borders, where it stood for many years. **NMS** IB 202.
    Front: equal-armed cross entirely and deliberately erased, set within border of interlace, spirals and

key-work. The background has four panels each containing fantastic beasts: (1) a pair of twisted bug-eyed serpents biting each other's bodies; (2) a monster with four legs and tail ending in a serpent's head swallowing a man (?Jonah and the Whale); (3) a pair of animals facing each other's hindquarters and biting their hindlegs above a thick and long-necked creature with its head in the mouth of another beast; (4) a deer-like animal with bug-eyes looking down on a monster with a tail ending in a serpent's head, and holding a dead beast by the hind leg in its mouth. Below, part of a beast's head. *Back:* top panel, a galloping horseman and double-disc above a step symbol. Traces of another horseman and other creatures, one a bull appear in the lower panel.

Pictish sites without stones

37 Turin Hill, Angus. NO 513 535. Three structures which seem to have been built chronologically.

38 Finavon Hill, Angus. NO 507 557. This may have been re-enforced at the same time as the building of the third structure at Turin Hill to guard a centre of power at Aberlemno.

39 Restenneth Priory is situated about a mile (1.6 km) north-east of Forfar at NO 482 516. Part of the tower was once thought to have survived from the first stone church dedicated to St Peter (*c.* 712) but is now shown to be of 11th-century origins. However Egglespether – Pictish for St Peter's Church – was thought to have been somewhere in this area. In 1161 Restenneth became an Augustinian Priory.

DEESIDE AND STONEHAVEN

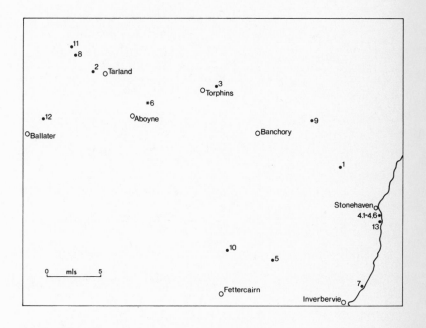

11
8
2 oTarland
3
oTorphins
6
12
oAboyne
9
oBallater
oBanchory
1
Stonehaven o
4.1-4.6
13
10
5
0   mls   5
7
Fettercairn o
Inverbervie o

1 Auquhollie NJ 823 907 8½ ft (259 cm) high stands in field near Auquhollie Farmhouse c.5 miles (0.8 km) north-west of Stonehaven.
Ogam inscription reads V U O N O N T E D O V.

2 Corrachree ✤ **C.I.** Whinstone. This stands in a field behind Corrachree House at NU 462 047.
PS: triskele in a disc at the top and the remains of two other unrecognisable symbols.

3 Cothill, Craigmyle House. ✤ **C.I.** Granite. 7½ ft (229 cm) tall. Slab which stands on rocky granite elevation north of the Dee on the south-west slope of the hill of Fare between Banchory and Aboyne at NJ 640 024.
PS: faint remains of a ?notched rectangle & Z-rod above a snake.

4 Dunnicaer, Stonehaven. ✤ Six stones **C.I.** c. 2 ft (61 cm). Found in an enclosure on top of an isolated rock-stack on the south side of Strathlethan Bay near Dunnottar Castle at NO 882 846. All except 4.4, which is in the **Anthropological Museum, Aberdeen,** are at Banchory House in the walled garden. NJ 915 024.

4.1: a double-disc & Z-rod roughly incised with unusual flourishes.

4.2: a salmon with a dot in a triangle above its head.

4.3: a crescent combined with an equilateral triangle.

4.4: ✤ a double-disc & Z-rod on one side with a flower, mirror and comb on the other.

4.5: two discs close together with dots in the centres, maybe meant to be a double-disc.

4.6: a cube-shaped fragment with incised images on all four faces.
Front: a circle with what looks like the end of a Z-rod.
Back: a circle and what looks like the letter R.
Right side: a small cross impinging on the side of an irregular circle, and a design that looks like a Q.
Left side: a design resembling that on the right side, but with a T combined with the circle as well as the cross.

5 Fordoun, Auchenblae. **C.II.** 5¼ ft tall (160 cm). Cross-slab sculptured part in relief, part incised, which stands in the vestibule of Fordoun church 10 miles (16 km) south-west of Stonehaven. NO 726 784.

Front: slab broken off through the middle of the top arm. Circular hollows between the arms deeply cut. Part of a seahorse in the top arm, knotwork in the left arm and centre of the cross with a mounted warrior holding a spear in lower arm. In the left top background, Hiberno-Saxon minuscules spell the name P I D A R N O I N. Two horsemen facing left with a hound and beast flank the central horseman. Below find a decorated double-disc & Z-rod.

Comment: St Palladius was known as 'the first apostle of Ireland'. He may have been buried here or his relics brought to the ancient chapel. St Palladius' Well was known for healing.

6 Formaston, Aboyne. ✤ **C.II.** Granite. 9th century. Found in St Adamnan's churchyard at Formaston at NJ 541 001. It was moved to the grounds of Aboyne Castle and later taken into **Inverurie Museum**.

Front: bottom right-hand corner of a cross-slab. The shaft is ornamented with interlace, and beading at the bottom is twisted into C-shaped spirals. Mirror to the right of the shaft.

Ogams: inscription on the right of mirror on the perpendicular stem appears to read M A Q Q O I T A L L U O R R A. A second inscription on stem line to the right of the first reads N A H H T R A O B B A C C A A N N E O O. This second inscription may have been added later, as Ogams are carved into the beading which edges the stone.

7 Kineff ✤ **C.III.** Cross-slab found in 1898 among a heap of stones in a churchyard. Kineff is on the east coast, some 3 miles (4.8 km) north-east of Inverbervie at NO 856 749. **NMS** IB 194.

Description: a cross in low relief with only the left arm and centre complete. It has rounded armpits and is decorated with bosses set in triangles.

8 Migvie C.II. Greenish gneiss. 6 ft (183 cm) high. Cross-slab which stands in the graveyard of Migvie Church, some 3½ miles (5.6 km) north-west of Tarland at NJ 437 068.

Front: interlaced cross has slightly expanded ends with six strange projections shaped like key-handles protruding from the top and angles. Background on the left shows a double-disc & Z-rod above shears; on the right an arch with V-rod above mounted man. *Back:* a man on horseback about 1¾ ft tall (53 cm).

9 Park House ✤ **C.I.** This once stood on Keith's Muir at *c.* NO 794 984. In 1821 it was removed and set on a pedestal in the grounds of Park House at NO 780 977.
PS: the remains of what may have been a notched rectangle & Z-rod above a crescent & V-rod with a mirror and comb beneath.

10 St Ringan's Cairn, Redstone Hill. ✤ **C.II.** Found in 1964 during the clearance of a pile of stones at NO 655 794. Lost.
PS: carved in high relief, one panel showed the body and hindquarters of a ?boar.

11 Tillypronie House (originally Mill of Newton, Tom a Char) ✤ **C.I.** Found 5 miles (8 km) north-west of Dinnet, built into a farmsteading wall at Mill of Newton, it is now at Tillypronie House 8 miles (12.9 km) north of Dinnet at NJ 432 080.
PS: a notched rectangle & Z-rod above a crescent and V-rod.

12 Tullich C.I. Blue slate. *c.*6 ft (182 cm) tall. Noticed by the minister of Dinnet in use as a lintel above a window in the north wall of the ruined church at Tullich before 1900, it is now placed within iron railings with other slabs bearing incised crosses at the north end of the ruins 5 miles (8 km) west of Dinnet on the A93. NO 391 975.
PS: a double-disc & Z-rod above a Pictish beast with a mirror below.

Pictish sites without stones

13 Dunnottar Castle, Kincardineshire. NO 882 839. An important stronghold with access for the Pictish navy.

ABERDEEN AND THE GRAMPIANS

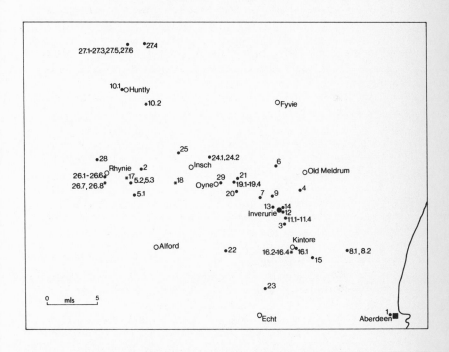

27.1-27.3,27.5,27.6 •27.4

10.1 OHuntly
•10.2
OFyvie

•25
•28 •24.1,24.2
Rhynie •2 OInsch •6 OOld Meldrum
26.1-26.6 O •17 29 •21
26.7, 26.8 * •5.2,5.3 •18 OyneO• •19.1-19.4
•5.1 20• •7 •9 •4
13• •14
Inverurie •12
•11.1-11.4
3•

OAlford Kintore
•22 16.2-16.4•• •16.1 •8.1, 8.2
•15

•23

0   mls   5
OEcht 1
Aberdeen■

1 The Anthropological Museum, Marischal College, University of Aberdeen, displays several symbol stones and other artifacts relating to the Picts. Here you will see the **Goose Stone 29.1** and **Wantonwells;** also **Collace, Fairy Green,** from Perth, and **Dunicaer 4.4** from Deeside.

OPEN: Weekdays 10am – 5pm and 2 – 5pm Sunday.

2 Ardlair of Kennethmont C.I. Grey-blue gneiss. This was noticed near the stone circle. It may have been a stone re-used by Picts. Situated *c.* 3 miles (4.8 km) beyond Rhynie on the B9002 south-east off the A97, 300 yards (274 m) south of Ardlair Farm at NJ 555 278.

PS: a Pictish beast beside a broken sword with a mirror below.

3 Broomend of Crichie C.I. This originally stood to the east of the stone circle in a field on Crichie Farm at NJ 780 197. It was later re-erected within a henge. It is said there were six stones with associated burial sites round the inside of a ditch with a seventh in the centre. All but two were removed for building purposes. The remaining two, with Crichie between them, can be found east off the A96 some 2 miles (3.2 km) north-west of Kintore at NJ 779 197.

PS: a Pictish beast above a crescent & V-rod.

4 Bourtie C.I. Blue whinstone. This is built into the outer wall of the church, high up at the east end of the south face. Turn right off the A96 in Inverurie and on to the B9170 and right again to Kirkton of Bourtie. NJ 805 249.

PS: a crescent & V-rod incised above a plain double-disc with a mirror and double-edged comb below. The left sides of the top symbols are missing and the stone is set incorrectly into the wall.

5 Clatt

5.1: ✤ C.I. Whinstone. 4½ ft (137 cm) tall. This was noticed in the old graveyard wall at Clatt NJ 539 260. It was built into a cottage close to the schoolhouse. When this was demolished, the stone was removed to Knockespock House 1½ miles (2.4 km) south of Clatt at NJ 544 241.

PS: a cauldron above a double-disc and part of a mirror.

5.2: ✤ C.I. Found *c.*1900 in the churchyard at Clatt NJ 538 260. Lost.

PS: parts of a double-disc & Z-rod.

5.3: C.I. Found in 1905 and built into the churchyard wall, south of the rear gate. NJ 538 260.
PS: parts of a Pictish beast and arch.

6 Daviot ✣ C.I. Whinstone. This was found embedded in the ground by the roadside almost opposite the farmhouse of Newton of Mounie at NJ 760 286, and was removed for preservation to Mounie Castle at NJ 767 286.
PS: a crescent and V-rod; below left, a mirror and single-edged comb with an unrodded crescent to the right.

7 Drimmies (Drummies) **C.I.** Red granite. 4 ft (122 cm) tall with the top missing. It has been built into a wall at the entrance to Drimmies Farm on the A96 *c.* 3 miles (4.8 km) north-west of Inverurie. NJ 743 235.
PS: tips of a broken arch at the top above an S-shaped symbol with a mirror and double-edged comb.

8 Dyce
8.1: C.I. Grey granite. 5½ ft (168 cm) tall. This is said to have been found on the glebe of the old Chapel of St Fergus and was built into the east wall of Dyce Church in 1890. NJ 875 154.
PS: a Pictish beast over a decorated double-disc & Z-rod.

8.2: C.II. Cross-slab found in the glebe of St Fergus' Chapel and now situated near Dyce 1 at NJ 875 154.
Front: a decorated cross with hollow armpits and a central medallion of spiral-work. The background is plain.
Back: left of the lower shaft, a crescent & V-rod above a cauldron. On the right a disc and rectangle decorated with concentric circles and double spirals above a double-disc & floriated Z-rod.

9 East Balhalgardy (Balhaggardy) ✣ **C.I.** This forms the lintel above a window in the old steading of East Balhalgardy Farm. NJ 761 238.
PS: a very worn double-disc or disc and traces of another symbol.

10 Huntly
10.1: C.I. One of the two **Standing Stones of Strathbogie** which were removed and placed in the market square at NJ 529 400, near the statute of the Duke of Richmond.

PS: part of a defaced arch above faint traces of a double-disc.

10.2: ✣ **C.I.** This was found in a field at the Leys of Drummies, Drumblade NJ 558 376. The farmer blasted it into two pieces, one of which may be buried in field. The other was noticed in 1882 and presented to Huntly Field Club. In 1903, it was lying in a Huntly garden until later acquired by **NMS** IB 179.
PS: part of a double-disc & Z-rod.

11 Inverurie Old Churchyard. There are four stones in the kirkyard under the railway bridge on the B993 close to an artificial mound called the Bass. NJ 780 206.

11.1: C.I. Damaged slab of red granite *c.* 6 ft (183 cm) long.
PS: from the top, a crescent & V-rod, a disc & rectangle, a snake & Z-rod, a double disc & Z-rod.

11.2: C.I. Rectangular fragment of red granite.
PS: possibly a mirror attached to an arch, or possibly a mirror with part of an elaborate handle.

11.3: C.I. Rectangular fragment of red granite.
PS: a small segment of a circle above a double-disc & Z-rod.

11.4: C.I. Triangular-shaped fragment of red granite.
PS: the incised figure of a trotting horse with scrolled muscles, pricked ears and mane. Some argue this may be a later carving associated with the horse cult known as 'The Horseman's Word', but not in my opinion. These scrolled muscles closely resemble other Pictish animal carvings, thus setting the carving firmly in the Pictish era.

12 Inverurie Museum, situated in the centre of town, holds a few Pictish stones worth visiting. These include **Kintore 16.4** and **Formaston** from Aboyne.

13 Inverurie, Brandsbutt. C.I. Whinstone. This was noticed in 1899 in a dyke dividing two fields west of a farm steading. When this was demolished, the other parts of the massive slab were found and fixed together. It is sign-posted on the A96 on the north side of town and stands in a new housing estate. NJ 760 224.
PS: a crescent & V-rod above a snake & Z-rod. Left of the symbols, an Ogam inscription reads I R A T A D D O A R E N S . . .

14 Keith Hall ✤ **C.I.** Whinstone. 5 ft (152 cm) tall. This was found in 1853 in the River Don and preserved in Keith Hall, north off the B993 just beyond the Bass at NJ 788 214, and is now placed on the homestead moat at Caskieben.
PS: a double-disc & Z-rod above a salmon with a mirror & comb at the bottom.

15 Kinellar C.I. Granite. *c*.3 ft (91 cm) high. This was found in 1801, forming the foundation of the south-east corner of the old church. NJ 821 145. It is now in the vestibule.
PS: three discs in a circle above a crescent & V-rod.

16 Kintore

16.1: C.I. Fine-grained granite. *c*. 3½ ft (107 cm) tall. It was found covering a grave in Kintore churchyard. NJ 793 163.
Front: a salmon above a cauldron.
Back: a crescent & V-rod above a Pictish beast.

16.2 and **16.3:** ✤ **C.I.** Red granite. 5 ft (152 cm) and 6½ ft (198 cm) tall. These were found near the church in Castle Hill, thought to be a prehistoric site at NJ 794 163. **NMS** IB 22 and IB 23.
16.2. *Front:* a Pictish beast above a double-disc & Z-rod.
Back: symbols are set in reverse position compared with front. A mirror above a Pictish beast. The snout of a beast erased on both sides.
16. 3. Two crescents back to back, their convex edges touching. A tuning-fork is on the right.

16.4: ✤ **C.I.** This was found in cleared garden top-soil in the early 70s. NJ 790 162. **Inverurie Museum**.
PS: A Pictish beast, a mirror and symbol showing two squares one within the other with opposite scalloped corners.

17 Leith Hall, Percylieu, Hillhead of Clatt ✤ **C.I.** Whinstone. Slab found at Percylieu Farm connected to the stone circle half a mile (0.8 km) north of Clatt At NJ 535 264. Gifted to the **NTS** in 1905, it is now kept in shelter on the north wall of **Leith Hall** garden. NJ 540 230.
PS: two fins of a fish above an arch.

18 Leith Hall, Newbigging Leslie ✤ **C.I.** Red granite. This was found *c*. 1842 while trenching farm land. Afterwards it was noticed in a dyke and put in a rockery behind the

farm at NJ 604 258. It was presented to **NTS** in 1905, and now stands beside **Percylieu** at **Leith Hall**.
PS: a rectangle above a wolf (similar to **Ardross Wolf** in Inverness Museum). Also a mirror & decorated single-edged comb.

19 Logie Elphinstone Stones, Pitcaple. ✤ Three surviving C.1 stones, found close together on Moor of Carden, west of Logie Elphinstone House *c.* 1821. They were subsequently erected in a garden. NJ 703 259.

19.1: ✤ C.I. Whinstone. 3½ ft (107 cm) tall.
PS: a crescent & V-rod, a double-disc.

19.2: ✤ C.I. Pointed pillar of whinstone, 4½ ft (137 cm) high.
PS: Ogam inscription on the circular stem-line; below a crescent & V-rod, above a double-disc & Z-rod. There are faint traces of another double-disc which may have been partly erased in order to incise the other symbols.

19.3: ✤ C.I. Rectangular slab of whinstone 3½ ft (107 cm) tall.
PS: a Pictish beast above a crescent & V-rod.

19.4: ✤ is said to have been used by a tenant as a hearth-stone in his kiln, and was split and destroyed.

20 Maiden Stone C.II. Red granite. 10 ft (305 cm) tall. Very worn. Take the side road to Chapel of Garioch off the A96 almost opposite Drimmies stone. The stone stands in remote and rising ground *c.* 1 mile (1.6 km) west of Garioch at NJ 704 247.
Front: divided into five panels: (1) above a cross find a man with arms outstretched and fish monsters with spiral tails on either side of him; (2) a ringed cross with round hollow armpits with all ornamentation defaced; in (3) and (4) no trace of sculpture remains; (5) spiral and knot-work decoration.
Back: four panels reading from the top: (1) several defaced beasts; (2) a notched rectangle & Z-rod. A triangular section has been broken off the stone between these top two panels on the right following a natural crack in the granite; (3) a Pictish beast and (4) a mirror & double-edged comb.
Both sides: decorated with very worn interlace.
Comment: The Maiden Stone is one of the few Class II cross-slabs to be found in Aberdeenshire and may

belong to the second half of the 9th century, thus post-dating the reign of Kenneth Mac Alpin. Political changes in the south may have had little immediate effect on the artistic traditions of the Picts here.

21 Mill of Lewesk ✤ C.I. Formerly at Logie House NJ 705 259 is recorded as lost.
PS: a double crescent, a disc & rectangle and rectangle & rod.

22 Monymusk C.II. 7 ft (213 cm) tall. Beautiful cross-slab carved in delicate relief on one side only. It once stood in a field east of Monymusk House near the River Don at NJ *c.* 703 151, then built into a recessed cupboard in the billiard room of Monymusk Castle. It is now in the local church. NJ 685 152.
 Front: a cross with round hollow armpits stands on a narrow shaft, rising from a small semi-circular base. There is varied decoration in seven panels. Below, find an elaborate step symbol and cauldron.

The Monymusk Reliquary, ✤ otherwise known as the **Brecbennoch of St Columba,** is thought to have contained some relic of that great man. It was carried as a standard strapped to the bearer's brow or breast in the Battle of Bannockburn. It was kept at Monymusk Castle for many centuries before being placed in the care of **NMS** Edinburgh, where you can see it today.

23 Nether Corskie C.I. This stands in a field south of Dunecht at NJ 748 096. It is thought to have come from a prehistoric stone circle and reused by the Picts.
PS: a very faint mirror & comb and disc & rectangle.

24 Newton House
 24.1: ✤ C.I. Blue gneiss. 6 ft 9 in (206 cm) tall. After two moves, this now stands in the grounds of Newton House where it was taken *c.* 1900. NJ 662 297.
 PS: a double-disc with small crescent-shaped notch taken out of the first disc above a snake & Z-rod.

 24.2: Newton House Ogham Stone ✤ Blue gneiss. Approximately the same height as Newton 24.1. It was first noticed in 1803 and stands close to Newton 24.1. There are no symbols but two inscriptions, one in Ogam, which seems to include the name E D D A R R N O N N among the letters. The other is in an unrecognised language. Many have written and speculated on the meaning of the script. It may have been carved in imitation of Irish majuscule script by an illiterate sculptor.

25 Picardy Stone, Insch **C.I.** Black whinstone slab with quartz veins. 6½ ft (198 cm) tall. It stands in a field at Myreton Farm at NJ 610 303. At Insch turn right on to the B992, then right again on the side-road to Largie until the stone is sighted. A path through the field is kept clear even if under crop.
PS: a double-disc & Z-rod, a snake & Z-rod with a mirror and possibly a comb below.

26 Rhynie
26.1 'The Craw Stane': C.I. This stands in a field about 100 yd (91 m) south of Rhynie village between the A97 and the Water of Bogie and nearly 5 miles (8 km) north of the junction of the A944 and the A97 at NJ 497 263.
PS: a salmon above a Pictish beast.

26.2 and **26.3 Plough Inn: C.I.** Whinstone. Both were identified *c*. 1836 in a field south of Rhynie at NJ 499 270. They now stand on the village green at NJ 498 272.
   26.2: a double-disc & V-rod, now invisible.
   26.3: a man's back, spear and disc.

26.4 Mains of Rhynie: ✤ **C.I.** 5 ft (152 cm) tall. This was found on the Mains of Rhynie at NJ 498 270. It was broken up but one part was built into a barn wall. The fragment disappeared when the barn was demolished before 1903. Lost.
PS: A Pictish beast above a half crescent & V-rod, a mirror but no comb.

26.5 and **26.6 Old Church: C.I.** Both were removed from the foundations of the original church when it was demolished in 1878, and are now at the entrance to the graveyard. NJ 499 265.
   26.5: a beast's head beside a double-disc & Z-rod placed vertically above a mirror and single-edged comb.
   26.6: part of a double-disc & Z-rod above a crescent & V-rod with a mirror below.

26.7 Rhynie Man: ✤ **C.I.** Found on a farm at Barflat in 1978 at NJ 498 264, this dressed slab contains a huge incised figure of an ogre with filed teeth, possibly tattooed brows and a strong nose with flared nostrils, carrying a rather flimsy axe. In Grampian Regional Council HQ, Woodhill House, Ashgrove Rd West, Aberdeen. NJ 912 072.

26.8 Rhynie Barflat: ✢ **C.I.** Pink granite. This was found by the plough in 1978 at NJ *c.* 498 263 and is now in Grampian Regional Council HQ. NJ 912 072.
PS: a Pictish beast, curvilinear symbol and comb.

27 The Tillytarmont Stones were all – except 28.4 – found on Donaldstone's Haugh at the junction of the Isla and the Deveron rivers at NJ 533 473.

27.1 'The Goose Stone': ✢ **C.I.** Bluish grey whinstone. This was found by the plough before 1867 on North Tillytarmont Farm. NJ 530 465. **Anthropological Museum, Aberdeen**.
PS: a goose above a mirror, disc & rectangle.

27.2: ✢ **C.I.** Red granite. Ploughed up in 1944 at NJ 533 472, and placed in Whitestones House at NJ 530 470.
PS: a crescent & V-rod, double-disc & Z-rod.

27.3: ✢ **C.I.** This was discovered about 1867 and redis-covered in 1954. Whitestones House.
PS: a crescent and double-disc & Z-rod.

27.4: ✢ **C.I.** Whinstone. This was found built into a dyke at North Redhill on Fourman Hill, at NJ 560 467. Whitestones House.
PS: a perpendicular rectangle with a semicircular notch at the lower end.

27.5: ✢ **C.I.** This was found in 1972 at NJ 533 472, and until recently stood in the garden of Little Craigherbs, Whitehills at NJ 652 647. **Anthropological Museum, Aberdeen**.
PS: a fine eagle above a Pictish beast.

27.6: ✢ **C.I.** Found by the plough in 1974 above spread of stones near cairn at NJ 533 472, this stone is now at the **Anthropological Museum, Aberdeen**.
PS: a snake & Z-rod, decorated arch and mirror & comb.

Pictish sites without stones

28 Tap o'Noth, Aberdeenshire. NJ 485 292. Huge timber-laced fort which has never been excavated and which has a massive vitrified wall. A series of hut-circles within an outer enclosure is thought to belong to the Pictish era.

29 Oyne Archaeolink Theme Park within a large housing estate is proposed for Oyne NJ 672 260 on the B9002. One of its purposes is to interpret and protect the stones in this area.

Moray
and Banff

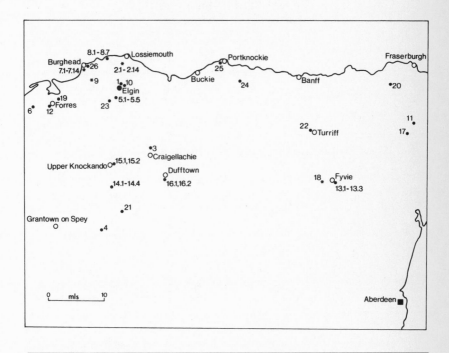

Burghead
7.1-7.14
8.1-8.7
Lossiemouth
26
2.1-2.14
Portknockie
25
Fraserburgh
9
Buckie
24
Banff
20
1
10
Elgin
5.1-5.5
19
Forres
6
12
23
11
22
Turriff
17
3
Craigellachie
Upper Knockando
15.1,15.2
Dufftown
14.1-14.4
16.1,16.2
18
Fyvie
13.1-13.3
21
Grantown on Spey
4

0   mls   10

Aberdeen

1 The Moray Society Museum, 1 High Street, Elgin IV30 1EQ, has an award-winning section devoted to Pictish artifacts and information. A huge collection of fragments, many of which came from the Pictish fortress of Burghead and many more from the early Christian site of Kinneddar excavated in 1978, are displayed or stored here.

2 Drainie, Kinneddar Manse
2.1: ✣ C.I. Fragment found while demolishing the manse in 1855. **The Moray Society Museum.**
PS: part of a crescent & V-rod.

2.2–13: ✣ C.III stones found in surrounding dykes and in the old churchyard are all preserved in **Elgin Museum.** Before Moray Cathedral was sited in Spynie, Kinneddar church was the seat of the diocese situated some 5 miles (8 km) north of Elgin on the B1935. NJ 223 696.

2.14: ✣ Fragments of a cross-slab showing a panel containing key-patterns, now in **NMS** IB 118.
Comment: Many more fragments were found in Kinneddar during excavations in 1978. The site is thought to have been a workshop where cross-slabs were manufactured.

3 Arndilly Stone ✣ C.I. Taken out of the wall of an old church on whose foundations Arndilly House was built, this stone is now set into a wall close to the house 2 miles (3.2 km) north of Craigellachie at NJ 291 471.
PS: a disc & rectangle set beside a notched rectangle & Z-rod.

4 Balneilean ✣ C.I. This is mentioned as having been sited in the wall of the farm offices in the parish of Knockando at NJ *c.* 149 259, but could not be located in 1971. Lost.
PS: a broken circular disc enclosing three small discs.

5 Birnie church, once the seat of the Bishop of Moray, stands on the east side of River Lossie 3 miles (4.8 km) south of Elgin Station. Cropmark photography has revealed a circular enclosure attached to the old church site. Five weathered fragments remain here at NJ 206 587.

5.1: C.I. Granite boulder with an eagle and notched rectangle & Z-rod.

5.2: C.III. Sandstone. Part of a cross-slab ornamented with a triple spiral and interlace. It is preserved in the church.

5.3: portion of the same cross-slab.

5.4: similar to the above.

5.5: similar, with traces of key-pattern.

6 Brodie Castle (Rodney's Stone) C.II. Grey sandstone. *c.* 6 ft (183 cm) high. Cross-slab found in the graveyard of the old church of Dyke and Moy. It was moved to the village of Dyke NH 990 584 to commemorate the victory of Admiral Rodney and now stands on the left side of the avenue leading to Brodie Castle at NH 984 577.

Front: a cross extends from the top to the bottom and is decorated with a continuous interlace pattern, worked in a series of different knots. Background, arranged in four panels, as follows: (1) above the left arm, a beast with a tail and legs interlaced. Badly defaced; (2) above the right arm, defaced; (3) left of the shaft, pairs of beasts mostly obliterated by the initials K.D., cut upside down into a recess; (4) right of the shaft, pairs of beasts with the initials A.C. cut upside down into a recess. On either side of the lower front find badly defaced Ogam letters on a stem line.

Back: a single panel showing, from the top, a pair of beautifully ornamented fish monsters or fanged seahorses facing each other with some curious circular objects between them. Below, find a Pictish beast with an ornamented body and a double-disc & Z-rod with similar distinctive decoration. Ogam inscriptions on raised bands forming the vertical sides of the panel are badly defaced. Only those on the bottom of the right side can be read and spell what seems to be a personal name, E D D A R R N O N   Q. A caste of the stone may be seen in Inverness Museum and a descriptive leaflet is available.

Burghead was once an important Iron-Age fortress in use during the Pictish era, and is the largest fortified site in early historic Scotland. NJ 109 691.

7 Burghead Bulls C.I. There may have been some 30 bull effigies of which six have survived as follows:

7.1: ✣ a perfect specimen. Bold incised lines show the scrolled muscles to perfection, while the swishing tail gives an impression of strength and fertility. This was allegedly found in the great well within the fortress and presented by Sir Thomas Dick Lauder to the Museum of Scientific Association, Inverness. In 1891 it was given to **NMS** IB 95.

7.2: similar to No.1, but the tail hangs limp. It is badly water-worn with the head almost defaced. Found in 1862 during alterations to the south quay, this is now in the care of Moray Museums Service and is displayed in the window of Burghead Library.

7.3: ✣ water-worn. It was found amongst rubbish in Burghead. **Elgin Museum**.

7.4: only the water-worn head and shoulders remain. It was found in 1867 while demolishing a house on the south quay. **Burghead Library**.

7.5: ✣ this was found before 1809 and is now in the **British Museum**.

7.6: ✣ only the water-worn front-half remains. It was found in 1854 during alterations to the south way and is now in **Elgin Museum.**
Comment: These bull slabs may have been thrown into the sea during the performance of some ritual. All show traces of water-wear, but this may be accidental rather than deliberate. Alternatively, they may have adorned the walls of the fortress.

Burghead Stones Besides the bull slabs, eight further **C.III** stones have been discovered in the Burghead area. These are thought to be part of an early Christian corner-post shrine, which probably stood against the wall of a chapel, which suggest that there may have been a monastery and possibly a cross-slab within the fortress.

7.7: a small rectangular sandstone slab showing two beasts attacking a stag with a smaller beast watching. This was found in 1891 in the coping of the old churchyard. **Burghead Library**.

7.8: ✣ part of a cross-slab found in debris at Burghead.
Front: part of the top arm of a cross ornamented with triple spirals on a background of interlace.
Back: the upper part of a warrior with spear and shield slung round his neck (see Dupplin warriors). **NMS** IB 95.

7.9: ✤ A fragment of sandstone, decorated with a key-pattern and found when digging near a headland. **Elgin Museum**.

7.10 and 7.10a: fragments containing key-patterns.

7.11: ✤ fragment of a cross-slab found by Hugh Young, owner of Burghead before 1903. It is grooved on two faces and sculptured in relief on the two other faces. **Elgin Museum**.

7.12: ✤ found by Hugh Young in 1891 near the end of the promontory. It shows part of a panel with a key-pattern. **Elgin Museum**.

7.13: ✤ found by Hugh Young in 1892 on the beach near the point of the promontory. Key-pattern. **Elgin Museum**.

7.14: found while digging foundations of a store at the north side of the harbour in 1895. This stone shows two panels with triangular interlace on one and key-pattern on the other. Hugh Young describes it as made of very hard Covesea sandstone which seems to have been in a fire and discoloured by great heat. 'The carving is very finely executed'. **Elgin Museum**.

8 Covesea Caves

The Sculptor's Cave is the largest and most impressive of the many caves eroded into the yellow sandstone cliffs between Hopeman and Lossiemouth Lighthouse. NJ 175 707. A cliff path leads from Lighthouse to Hopeman with steps cut into the rocks to allow access to cave. (If you go by the shore be careful not to get cut off by the tide.) Continue west along the shore till you find the Sculptor's Cave, which is huge and dry and covered with inscriptions, signatures and graffiti. Take a torch to examine the interior. There are Pictish symbols near the two entrances to the cave.

8.1: east of the east entrance passage, a fish on its tail near a crescent & V-rod.

8.2: west of the east entrance near the roof, two pentacles side-by-side.

8.3: east of the west entrance, a triple oval.

8.4: west wall of the entrance, a crescent & V-rod, step symbol, double rectangle and two discs & rectangles.

8.5: on the roof between the two entrances, a triple oval and flower.

8.6: high on the east side of the west entrance, confused markings with a large mirror and crescent.

8.7: west side of the west entrance: a small crescent, possibly with a V-rod.
Comment: The cave is thought to have been a ritual site serving Burghead fortress during the Pictish era.

9 Easterton of Roseisle ✦ C.I. Found in 1894 by the plough, it formed the west side of an irregular stone cist *c.* 3 miles (4.8 km) south-east of Burghead at NJ *c.* 144 647. **NMS** IB 226.
Front: from the top, a crescent with an arch-shaped indentation on lower edge, a crescent & V-rod, mirror & comb.
Back: a goose above salmon, both beautifully carved.

10 Elgin Cathedral C.II. Grey granite containing felspar crystals. *c.* 7 ft (213 cm) high. Cross-slab found in 1823 during street repairs near St Giles Church at NJ 216 629. It now stands within the ruined cathedral at NJ 222 631.
Front: a cross with badly-worn interlace, small hollow armpits and a central circular boss. The background has four panels: (1) and (2) two winged, haloed figures with books or book satchels round their necks. The figures represent two Evangelists; (3) the left panel shows a bearded, moustached Matthew with a halo and symbol of a Man looking over his shoulder; (4) the right panel shows a similar figure with a book but no halo, and an Eagle of St John above his right shoulder. Below the base of the cross are four intertwined beasts biting each other's bodies.
Back: a single panel, reading from top, shows a spiral decoration, ornamented double-disc & Z-rod, crescent & V-rod, hunting scene with hounds attacking stag, and four mounted huntsmen, the first of whom has a hawk on his outstretched arm with a ?grouse in front of the horse.

11 Fetterangus C.I. Water-worn whinstone. 3 ft 8 in (112 cm) high. Slab fixed to the old churchyard wall at the right of the entrance. NJ 981 506.
PS: a curved line ending in small scroll above a disc & rectangle with a cauldron below.

12 Forres ✤ **C.I.** fragment found built into a garden wall in St Leonard's Road *c.* 1991. NJ 039 588. **Forres Museum**.
PS: part of an incised crescent & V-rod.

13 Fyvie

13.1 C.I Whinstone. *c.* 2½ ft (76 cm) by 2 ft (61 cm). Very worn symbol stone recognised in the outer wall of a tailor's shop, which was thereafter built into the church wall. NJ 769 378.
PS: part of a crescent & V-rod, a Pictish beast with a mirror with crescent-shaped end to the left of the snout.

13.2 C.I Whinstone. 2½ ft (76 cm). Symbol stone built into the exterior wall of the church.
PS: the right half of a double-disc above the middle portion of eagle.

13.3 C.III. Red granite. *c.* 5 ft (152 cm) high. Narrow pillar built into the exterior wall of the church below 13.2.
Front: two panels; (1) a distorted key-pattern and (2) triangular interlace with circular dots in triangles.

14 Inveravon: Four **C.I** stones discovered in the foundations of the old church situated on the south east bank of the Spey a mile (1.6 km) south of the junction with the Avon at Blacksboat. They are mounted on the outside of the south wall of the present church at NJ 183 376.

14.1: a slab of blue slate. *c.* 5 ft (152 cm) high.
PS: a decorated disc with notched rectangle set on the half-segment of a circle above an eagle and mirror & comb.

14.2: a slab of gneiss or whinstone *c.* 5 ft (152 cm) long.
PS: from the top, a crescent & V-rod, cauldron, mirror & comb.

14.3: a rectangular block of hard blue gneiss.
PS: the head of a Pictish beast.

14.4: a large slab of metamorphosed sandstone, found in 1964.
PS: an incised crescent & V-rod, and a Pictish beast.

15 Knockando Church C.I. Two stones said to have been taken from the old burial ground of Pulvrenan are now built into a wall at Knockando churchyard entrance, situated north of the River Spey and 3 miles (4.8 km) north of Blacksboat off the B9012 at NJ 187 429.

15.1: a slab of gneiss *c.* 5 ft (152 cm) high.

PS: a disc with lines radiating from a central concentric circle (similar to a spoked wheel) above two crescents, side-by-side, the first of which has a V-rod.

15.2: a slab of dioritic stone over six feet (183 cm) tall.
PS: a snake above a mirror.

16 Mortlach

16.1 Mortlach 'Battle Stone': C.II. Green slate. 6 ft (183 cm) high. Cross-slab, which once stood on the west bank of Dullan Water on the south outskirts of Dufftown. NJ 324 392. It is now in Mortlach churchyard.

Front: carved in relief this shows two fish monsters facing each other above a cross containing crudely-carved spirals. Below, a curious little beast with three toes on each of its four short legs.

Back: faint traces of an incised eagle at the top above a snake and a bull's head with a huntsman and hound at the bottom.

16.2: C.I. This was found in 1925 and built into the vestibule of the church. NJ 324 393.
PS: a Pictish beast and a curvilinear symbol.

17 Old Deer ✛ C.I. 6 ft (183 cm) tall. This once stood at the end of a group of buildings attached to the ancient Cistercian Abbey of Deer to which the famous manuscript Gospel Book of Deer once belonged. NJ 968 481. Lost.

Front: a rectangle above a crescent & V-rod. Both ornamented.

Back: an outline cross placed in reverse position to the symbols.

Comment: The Book of Deer was discovered in Cambridge University Library in 1860. Its importance lies in the Gaelic notations which date from the 11th and 12th centuries and refer to grants of land to an unnamed religious house which was presumably Deer. Of the Abbey itself only some ruins remain.

18 Rothiebrisbane ✛ C.I. Whinstone. A symbol stone found near Rothiebrisbane House NJ 745 378 and placed in the garden. It is now at Fyvie church. NJ 769 378.

PS: three circles in a disc similar to Kinellar.

19 Sueno's Stone C.III. ORS. 20 ft (610 cm) high. Cross-slab at the east end of Forres which demands attention

and inspires awe. It is undoubtedly one of the finest examples of Dark Age sculpture in Europe and should not be missed. No one knows why or when it was created or who commissioned it. The first references to it come in the early 18th century but it must have lain underground for centuries before then. It now stands on a grass lawn protected by a glass cage at NJ 046 595.

Front: dominated by a ringed cross with a very long shaft on a rectangular base. The background is divided into 11 panels. (1) to (8) round the head of the cross are too defaced to describe. (9) and (10) on either side of the shaft and on the shaft itself is knot-work interlace. (11) two tall men facing each other bend over a seated figure with two smaller figures in the corners. Dr Anthony Jackson suggests this might show the coronation of Kenneth MacAlpin.

Back: shows 98 figures divided into four panels as follows: Panel (1) a row of figures facing forwards and holding swords standing above eight mounted warriors divided into three rows and facing left; panel (2) five warriors facing forwards. The central figure seems to be wearing a kilt (Kenneth?). The second row shows eight men with central pair fighting. The third row shows six severed heads under a Celtic bell with clapper and, to the left six headless corpses, while a man below is severing a seventh head. Below, find two couples engaged in hand-to-hand fighting. The fourth row depicts three columns of mounted warriors fleeing from two columns of fighting foot soldiers. Panel (3) on the left shows three pairs of warriors, one above the other in single combat, matched by three pairs on the right, while in the middle, under a canopy or a bridge, find a group of torsos beside the group of severed heads which seems to amount to seven. Below the corpses, two pairs of men appear to be commenting on the scene above them. Panel (4) shows two rows of eight warriors all facing left with the four leading soldiers in both columns unarmed, possibly even roped or chained together like POWs followed by their victors with shields and swords.

Right edge: decorated with foliage and intertwining beast heads which are very worn and, at the bottom, the heads of two humans.

Left edge: pairs of beasts, zoomorphic interlace, four mermaids or men with fish-like tails interlaced into figures-of-eight and, at the bottom, three men with their heads only visible.

Comment: It is generally accepted that this stone commemorated a battle, possibly two. Dr Jackson is convinced – and his argument is very credible – that the stone was erected by Kenneth Mac Alpin in the 9th century to inform the Picts of Moray in symbolic language that they were conquered, their king dead, and that it was no use fighting back. In short: Scotland rules, okay?

20 Tirie C.I. Blue mica schist. 3 ft 8 in (112 cm) high. Symbol stone which was taken out of the foundations of an old parish church and built into an inside wall next to the vestry. It is just off the A 98 about 5 miles (8 km) south-west of Fraserburgh. NJ 930 631.

PS: An eagle above a notched rectangle & Z-rod. The same combination as Birnie in Moray.

21 Tom na Heron ✛ C.I. This once stood in a field *c.* 3 miles (4.8 km) south of Inveravon at NJ 208 310. Lost.

PS: A snake and other symbols.

22 Turriff Manse C.I. Sandstone. 1 ft 8 in (51 cm) long. This slab is built into the inside of the north wall of old manse garden at NJ 723 499. Some 10 miles (16 km) north of Fyvie on the A947.

PS: part of a crescent & V-rod.

23 Upper Manbean C.I. Gneiss specked with fine mica. *c.* 3 ft (91 cm) high. Half of the back has been split off. It stands in the 'Field of the Standing Stone' west of River Lossie, some 4 miles (6.4 km) south of Elgin off the B1910 at NJ 187 576.

PS: a horizontal beast with a fish body, tail, fins and a dog-like head above a double-sided mirror & comb.

Comment: At the top front above the symbols find initials M with H and S below. The break at the back of the stone may have happened when the initials T S P were cut.

Pictish sites without Stones

24 Gaulcross, Banffshire. A silver hoard was found in 1840 in this Bronze-Age ring cairn containing a pin, chain and bracelet. NJ 535 639.

25 Portknockie, Castle Hill, Banff. NJ 488 687. A timber-laced fortress from which Pictish kings ruled the land and had important access to the sea.

26 Burghhead, Moray. NJ 108 694. This, the largest of all the strongholds used by the Picts, was surrounded by a timber-laced rampart fixed with iron dowels. Radio-carbon dating suggests its erection was about AD 300. Inside is a well which may have been Pictish. Twenty steps lead down to a rock-cut chamber containing a central tank. Its uses may have been ceremonial, pagan and later Christian.

INVERNESS AND NAIRN, BADENOCH AND STRATHSPEY

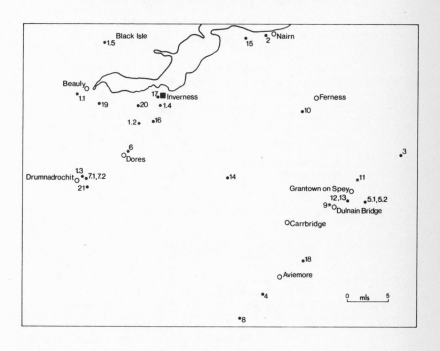

Black Isle
*1.5
15
2 ○Nairn

Beauly○
*1.1
•19   •20   17.■ Inverness
*1.4
○Ferness
•10

1.2• •16

*6
○Dores

Drumnadrochit○ 1.3
•*7.1,7.2
21•
•14
•11
Grantown on Spey○
12,13• •5.1,5.2
9*○Dulnain Bridge

•3

○Carrbridge

•18

○Aviemore

•4
0   mls   5

•8

Inverness was once the seat of Brude mac Maelcon, high king of the Picts, from *c.* 550-584. Some connect the hill-fort at Craig Phadraig with him, others Castle Urquhart on Loch Ness, but the most likely site of his palace was Castle Hill in the heart of the city, above the River Ness, where the present castle stands. Some believe him to have been responsible for establishing the Class I Pictish Stones, but there is no evidence of this.

1 Inverness Museum and Art Galleries, Castle Wynd, has an excellent Pictish interpretation which includes a number of Pictish artifacts and displays, including a caste of the Brodie Stone from Moray and the following Class I stones described below.

1.1 Beauly, Wester Balblair. ✤ **C.I.** Sandstone. This stone was found in a garden at Beauly in 1969. NH 510 453. **Inverness Museum** 1980.14.
PS: a triple oval and crescent & V-rod.

1.2 Cullaird, Scaniport. ✤ **C.I.** A fragment which was ploughed up on Cullaird farm in 1955 at NH 634 404. **Inverness Museum** 1955.30.
PS: possibly a mirror & comb, arch and rectangle and Z-rod.

1.3 Garbeg ✤ **C.I.** Sandstone. This was found excavating a cairn cemetery in 1974. NH 511 323. **Inverness Museum** 1974.75.
PS: a crescent & V-rod.

1.4 Kingsmills ✤ **C.I.** Sandstone. 1 ft (30 cm) high by 1 ft (30 cm) long. It was found before 1903 as stepping stone to a byre. NH *c.* 67 44. At **Stoneyfield House** NH 690 456.
Front: a bovine creature thought to be a bull.

1.5 Torgorm ✤ **C.I.** This was ploughed up on the farm of that name in the Black Isle, Ross-shire. NH *c.* 559 549. **Inverness Museum** 1937.41.
PS: parts of a double-disc & Z-rods.

1.6 Little Ferry Links ✤ **C.I.** From Golspie. No records. When compared with the stone in Dunrobin Castle (Sutherland District) the left side of a crescent & V-rod exactly matched the **Inverness Museum** portion.

1.7 The Ardross Wolf ✤ **C.I.** This famous fragment was found in 1903, built into a wall at Stittenham, Ardross, Ross &

Cromarty at NH *c.* 650 742. **Inverness Museum** 00.209.
PS: A wolf symbol.

1.8 The Ardross Deer ✤ slab was found with the Wolf
Stone in 1903. Some suggest that the two symbols were
once part of the same stone. **Inverness Museum** 00.208.
There are casts of both stones in Groam House Museum,
Rosemarkie.

2 **Achareidh House** ✤ C.III. Sandstone. Cross-slab fragment found in 1891 by workmen digging a post-hole. It is
decorated with a key pattern. NH 867 565.

3 **Advie** C.I. A fragment found in the old burial ground of
Advie in 1906. It is now set into the north wall of the
church. NJ 127 343.
PS: part of a crescent & V-rod, a disc and rectangle.

4 **Badenoch EC.** Mica schist. Just over a foot (30 cm)
square, a simple incised cross-slab with arrow-head
motifs on the arms that link into a circle. It was found in
1991 lying upside down over a drain at the south-west
corner of St Drosten's Parish Church, Alvie. NH 864 094.

5 **Congash**
5.1 and **5.2: C.I.** Blue gneiss. These two stones were
found on Congash Farm on the south bank of the Spey
c. 2 miles (3.2 km) east of Speybridge at NJ 058 262. They
form the jambs of the entrance to what was once a
kirkyard called *Parc an Caipel* – Field of the Chapel (also
known as the Field of Horses). Both stones have sunk
considerably so that only the upper symbols can be
clearly seen.
PS: 5.1: an arch above a Pictish beast.
PS: 5.2: a double-disc & Z-rod above a helmet or arrow
symbol.

6 **Dores,** Clune Farm. ✤ C.I. This was found during land
reclamation and built into a farm cottage as a chimney
head at NH *c.* 605 354. It is now in **NMS** IB 38.
PS: three legs and the middle of a ?boar with scrolled
joints.

7 **Drumbuie**
7.1 and **7.2:** ✤ C.I. Chocolate-coloured sandstone. These
were discovered in 1864 on Drumbuie Farm on the north

side of Urquhart Bay. These formed the covering of a cist-like burial construction. NH 515 312. **RMS** IB 287 & 288.
PS: **7.1**: a snake & Z-rod above a double-disc.
PS: **7.2**: the tail of a fish symbol above a disc and rectangle, mirror & comb.

8 Dunachton C.I. Diorite. Found in 1870 just west of Loch Insh near Kincraig, this stone formed the lintel above the door of the old steading demolished to provide stones to build Dunachton Lodge. It was seen in 1993 beside a walled garden at NH 821 046.
PS: a beast's head symbol.
Comment: Dunachton gets its name from Nechtan, a common Pictish name, which in this case may possibly be linked with King Nechtan mac Derile who, in the early 8th century, established the Pictish Church. Near Newtonmore on the River Calder, a bangor or monastery once stood, as the place-name Glen of Banchor indicates. The monastic site so far has not been identified.

9 Finlarig ✤ C.I. Mica schist. 3½ ft (107 cm) tall. This was found on a farm 2 miles (3.2 km) south-west of Grantown Station. It was dug up on the west side of a circular enclosure within which was a ruined chapel. NH *c.* 991 253. **NMS** IB 11.
PS: a small part of a rectangle & Z-rod, half of a crescent & V-rod.

10 Glenferness or **The Prince's Stone** ✤ C.II. Soft sandstone with veins of quartz which stand out in relief. 5½ ft (168 cm) tall. This stone originally stood under an ash tree growing on a small cairn close to the east bank of Findhorn River. In the late 50s it was moved to NH 937 426 about 300-4OO yd (275-366 m) from the house to protect it from possible flooding. It is very worn.
Front top panel: a cross with circular hollow arm-pits connected by a narrow ring with a short shaft.
Front lower panel: two men with heads over each other's shoulders embracing or wrestling.
Background, spiral work.
Back top panel: interlace too defaced to decipher.
Back lower panel: a kneeling figure shooting with cross-bow similar to Shandwick, St Vigeans 1 and Meigle 27.10. Behind the archer on the right, a Pictish beast and crescent & V-rod. Below, find a

leaping hound and a double-disc & Z-rod. Below again, another Pictish beast.
Edges: originally decorated with interlace but now obliterated by support posts.

11 Grantown-on-Spey ✧ **C.I.** Mica schist. This was found on the north bank of the Spey while digging in a mound known as Freuchie's Hillock. NJ 045 301. **NMS** IB 10.
PS: a stag with spiral joints and a full head of antlers above a rectangle.
Comment: This is one of the finest Pictish animal carvings and the only stag to be used as a symbol.

12 Inverallan C.I. Blue slate. 3½ ft (168cm) long. Slab found during the demolition of an old church dedicated to St Peter. Find the stone embedded in the boundary wall of the cemetery about 2 miles (3.2 km) south-west of Grantown at NJ 027 260. Cast in **NMS** IB 97.
PS: a crescent & V-rod, notched rectangle & Z-Rod.

13 Inverallan Cross known as Figgat's Cross, stands in the centre of the burial ground. It is thought to be Pictish.

14 Invereen ✧ **C.I.** A slab unearthed by the plough in 1932 at NH 797 311. **NMS** IB 227.
PS: crescent & V-rod, double-disc & Z-rod.

15 Kebbuck Stone, Delnies. ✧ *c.* 5 ft (152 cm) high. Badly weathered cross-slab found on the farm at Wester Delnies 4 miles (6.4 km) west of Nairn and north of the road to Ardersier. NH 826 555.

16 Knocknagael Boar Stone C.I. Hard slate. This stood in a field some 3 miles (4.8 km) south of Inverness at NH 657 413. In 1991 it was conserved and removed to the Highland Region Council Chambers, Glenurquhart Road, Inverness. Access is during Council hours.
Front: a disc & rectangle above a superb boar. Note the curved joints similar to the Ardross wolf and the Burghead bulls.

17 Lochardil slab ✧ was found in an old dyke near Provost Ross's house at Lochardil NH 665 438. It was kept in the stables there before its removal to Stoneyfield House NH 690 456.
Description: possibly a long-horn cow.

18 Lynchurn ✧ C.I. Slaty stone. This was first found in a field at Lynchurn Farm on the west bank of the Spey *c.* 1 mile (1.6 km) north of Boat of Garten. Moved, defaced and used as tombstone in Kincardine kirkyard, where it was noted in 1895 at NH 938 155. It could not be found in 1991, and presumably is no longer recognisable.
PS: a crescent & V-rod.

19 Moniack ✧ C.I or II. 4½ ft (137 cm) tall. This stone stood west of the old Parish Kirk of Kilmorack near Balblair at NH 494 444, and in 1903 taken to Moniak Castle grounds at NH 552 436.
Description: a man walking with a club or sword. The folds of his clothing and tops of stockings are clearly incised. He may have a bird-head or wear a bird-mask. The cup-marks and decoration are almost obliterated by lichen.

Pictish sites without stones

20 Craig Phadraig, Inverness. NH 640 452. A timber-laced hill-fort, thought by some to have belonged to King Brude mac Maelcon in the 6th century.

21 Castle Urquhart, Loch Ness. NH 531 286. This is another contender for the site of King Brude's royal palace in the 6th century from the description in St Adamnan 'Life of St Columba'.

EASTER AND
WESTER ROSS

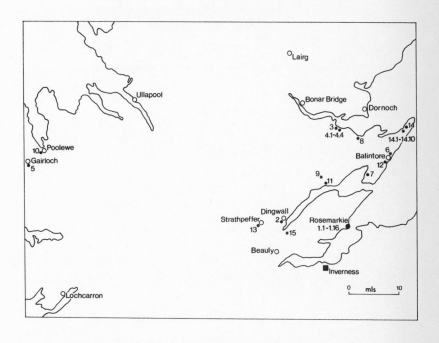

1 Groam House Museum and Pictish Centre, High Street, Rosemarkie IV10 8UF. Tel: 01381 620961.

OPEN: Daily May 1 to Oct 1, 10am – 5pm. Sunday afternoons. Every weekend afternoon throughout the winter.

This award-winning centre contains 15 C.II & III stones most of which were found in the vicinity of the Rosemarkie church – thought to be the site of the old monastery allegedly founded by St Curadan-Boniface in the early 8th century. Casts, display boards, videos, a playable Pictish-style harp, facilities for rubbing replicas and guides are available on request.

1.2 Rosemarkie Cross-slab: ✚ **C.II.** Local red sandstone. 9½ ft (290 cm) high with approximately 8 in (20 cm) missing from the top. *c.* 750 – 800. It was found in the floor of the original church either in the 18th or 19th century (records are unclear). It was broken in two pieces by the first removers (allegedly) and left in the kirkyard until mended and erected at the church door before placement in the museum in 1980. NH 737 576. This magnificent stone is the centre-piece of Groam House.

Front: three panels reading from the top; (1) linked rosettes of circular knotwork surrounding a plain equal-armed cross set in square panel. Deeply recessed squared armpits contain a key-pattern and spirals. Small indentations on the cross may have held jewels or reliquary; (2) filled with worn but superb zoomorphic interlace; (3) knotwork.

Back: three panels reading from the top; panel (1) left side edge of a crescent and apex of the rod; the remainder is broken off. Underneath on both sides find two long-necked beasts biting their own back legs with interlaced tails. The central crescent & V-rod is decorated with delicate key pattern. Unusually the V-rod is set behind the crescent. The central double-disc contains 17 bosses each of which displayed small spirals, now defaced, while the rod is floriated along its upper line. Between this and the lower crescent find a worn double-edged comb. Within the corners of the lower and most decorated crescent find the heads of two beasts at either end, each with fanged open jaws biting a serpent. All four serpentine bodies are interlaced within the crescent. Below, two mirrors or a mirror and case. Panel (2), an equal-armed cross with stepped ends, surrounded by four raised bosses. The design is thought to have

come from a 6th-century Persian Christian Manuscript. The background is filled with plait-work. *Side edges:* both contain panels of varied serpentine creatures and foliage with knotwork, spirals and triangles.
Comment: These elaborate symbols have declined from the simple original C.I form and could be interpreted as heraldic devices representing the local ruling family who may have commissioned the stone in memory of a king (?Nechtan) or possibly St Curadan/Boniface himself.

1.2 and **1.7**: ✤ **C.III.** Grey sandstone. Two recumbent slabs found in the graveyard. They are superbly carved in key patterns and spirals on one side only and are possibly parts of a box shrine containing relics of some important cleric, perhaps Curadan/Boniface. Sixteenth-century sources record that relics of Boniface/Curadan and his family (brother monks) were enshrined in the church. Alternatively, the slabs could have been screen panels attached to the interior of first church.

1.3 The Daniel Stone: ✤ **C.III.** Sandstone. Small fragment of (possibly) a cross-slab found in the churchyard *c.* 1885. It is carved on one side with four feet of a beast above the head of monster attacking the profiled head of a man. There are the heads of two more beasts to the right and below the man, who seems unlikely to be Daniel. Groam House displays a caste. **NMS** IB 127.

1.4 Two Ecclesiastics or **King with Servant:** ✤ **C.III.** Small fragment of a cross-slab dug up in the churchyard in 1885 showing the lower parts of two figures holding staffs or spears. Compare this with the kings on Birsay Stone from Orkney in NMS Edinburgh. On loan from **NMS**.

1.5 Border Fragment: ✤ **C.III.** Plain piece found in the churchyard in 1885, showing a border of interlace with the right side-edge decorated with a four-cord plait. On loan from **NMS**.

1.6 Ringed Cross: ✤ **C.III. ORS.** Beautiful fragment or complete stone carved possibly as an ornament for the interior of the church. ?Medieval. Holes in the centre and arms of cross possibly held precious stones. On loan from **NMS**.

1.8 Tree of Life Fragment: ✤ **C.III.** Grey-gold sandstone. Possibly the end of a box shrine with a groove on the back. The highly stylised vine is topped by a small cross, while branches are arranged in spirals separated by – and tipped with – pellets symbolising grapes.

1.9 Courthill Fragment: ✤ C.III. Upper part of a plain ringed cross with intertwining snakes above the upper arms. It was found in a Rosemarkie rockery in 1977 and is on loan from Inverness Museum.

1.10, 1.11 and **1.12: Plain Incised Crosses: ✤ EC.** Simple incised crosses, two of which may have been joined to form a recumbent gravestone.

1.13 Saltire Slab: ✤ C.III. Possibly part of a cross-slab. It was found in a rock garden in Fortrose in 1989. Badly mutilated and defaced.
Description: two pairs of legs and scrolled bodies with defaced heads within the border which surrounds a panel containing a saltire interlaced at the centre with triquetras between the arms.

1.14 Ringed Cross: ✤ C.III. Red sandstone. This was excavated in Rosemarkie kirkyard in 1990. It is an exquisitely sophisticated equal-armed ring cross on a rectangular pedestal. The top and left arms are broken off but the right arm is decorated with two spirals that extend out of the beading to touch the edge of the right arm.

1.15 and **1.16: ✤** Two new fragments, as yet unnamed, found in a Rosemarkie rockery in 1994. One shows a fragment of probably Pictish interlace. The other may be part of a 13/14th century medieval gravestone.

2 Dingwall C.I. Mica schist. 4¼ ft (137 cm) tall. This stone is probably a pre-Pictish monolith to be seen in St Clement's kirkyard, close to the entrance gate at NH 549 589.
Front **PS**: a double-disc & Z-rod; two crescents with V-rods.
Back **PS**: three discs above a crescent & V-rod. Also possibly six scattered cup-marks.

3 Edderton Salmon (*Clach Biorach* or The Sharp-pointed Stone) C.I. ORS. 10¼ ft (312 cm) high. Monolith situated in a field north of the village in line with a prehistoric stone circle which once contained a cist burial. NH 708 851.
PS: an incised salmon and verticle double-disc & Z-rod. Monolith clearly re-used by Picts.

Comment: This stone is still visited at solstices to see sunlight pour through notches between the Ardross Hills.

4 Edderton Churchyard C.III. Red sandstone. Originally 6 ft 3 in (191 cm) high. This cross-slab stands in the church-yard on the south side of the disused church. NH 719 843.
Front: an equal-armed, ringed cross separated by a bar from the long shaft, with five circles, one in the centre and four in the hollows of the arms.
Back: an equal-armed cross on a shaft which rises from a curved base (?Calvary), in which find one horseman without weapons. Below, and partially underground, find two armed, mounted warriors. The stone is badly defaced by lichen and weathering.

Four Edderton fragments. In August 1992, four fragments of what would seem to be another C.II or III cross-slab, or possibly two slabs, were rediscovered in a dump of red sandstone pieces, which may have been part of a collapsed building close to the church. The larger two were originally found lying under the turf in about 1900 and were thought to be parts of two separate cross-slabs as the borders did not match.

The **First fragment** is *c.* 3 ft (91 cm) tall by 2 ft (61 cm) wide. The arms of the equal-armed cross are badly defaced but were probably filled with interlace. Below is a bird with a hooked beak suggesting an eagle.

The **Second fragment** is so badly defaced that the sculpture has almost gone except for some inhabited vine-scrolling similar to Hilton of Cadboll.

Fragments 3 and 4 are tiny pieces of decorated stone found in 1993.

These fragments will hopefully be displayed after conservation in the disused Kincardine (Ardgay) Church or the nearest suitable museum.

5 Gairloch C.I. Slab on display at **Gairloch Museum and Heritage Centre**. NG 799 772.
PS: the lower part of an eagle above a beautifully carved salmon.

6 Hilton of Cadboll ✤ C.II. Red sandstone. Height 7 ft 9 in (236 cm). 8th century. This cross-slab originally stood by the chapel dedicated to St Mary the Virgin, close to the shore beyond Hilton. NH 873 769. **NMS** IB 189.

History: It was found face down on the seashore in 1811, and used in 1676 as a gravestone. Discovered in a shed attached to the ancient ruined church of Hilton. It was later removed to Invergordon Castle, then to the British Museum from whence – due to local uproar – it was returned in badly weathered and defaced condition to Edinburgh. The Hilton site itself is worth a visit.

Front: defaced.

Back: three panels set within a surrounding frame. A double-disc & small Z-rod placed within the top edge of the frame. The frame contains inhabited vine-scrolling where foliage may symbolise the Tree of Life with a marvellous selection of birds, representing the human soul feeding upon fruit. Panel (1) a crescent & V-rod decorated with knot-work and spirals separated by the two arms of the V-rod. Note the beautiful triple spiral at the angle of the rod. Below find two expanded discs ornamented with interlace; Panel (2) shows spirals in interlaced bosses similar to Shandwick; Panel (3) contains one of the few women to feature in Pictish art. She holds a more important position than the man who rides parallel to her but behind her. His bearded profile is visible to the left of the woman's head. Note the mirror & comb to the left of her horse's head. To her right, a leaping hound with two huntsmen blowing long horns. Below, two warriors in full battle-dress canter above a hind who is being attached by two leaping hounds.

Comment: This is perhaps the most discussed panel in Pictish art. Who is the woman? What is she holding? Why full-faced rather than profiled? Why do the hunters carry shields on the hunting field? What is the symbolism behind the scene? Perhaps it symbolises flight from evil with salvation in the church. The woman may be Mary holding the Christ-child with Joseph behind her in the Flight into Egypt. The hind may be the human soul in the Divine Hunt fleeing from the hounds and forces of evil. Safety is found within the branches of the Tree of Life, which represents the Cross of Christ. Some see the woman as holding a hawk on her arm, others as wearing a penannular brooch similar to the Denoon stone in The Meffan Institute, Forfar.

7 Nigg C.II. Grey sandstone. 7¼ ft (221 cm) high. 8th century. Cross-slab in Old Parish Church, Nigg. Missing panel lost. **PS**: An eagle and a Pictish beast. NH 805 717.
Front pediment: shows hermit-saints, Anthony and Paul, miraculously fed on a loaf of bread by a crow in the Syrian desert. The scene symbolises the Eucharist. *Front:* the arms of a cross contain serpent mazes surrounding a square panel of circular knotwork. These serpent mazes are seen as symbols to protect the centre of the cross which represents Christ. Note the delicate snake bosses in the central side panels. *Back:* set within 12 panels of exquisite interlace (two of which are incised), find four badly worn scenes. A drawing in **ECMS** roughs out what they may represent as follows; (1) an eagle and Pictish beast, most of which is lost in the missing panel; (2) a warrior with a spear, sword and shield following two hinds; (3) King David as shepherd and psalmist with sheep and harp, rending the lion's jaws; (4) a mounted hunter with hound and hind; also a man with two circular discs who looks as if he is clashing two cymbals.

8 Meikle Ferry, Tain ?C.I. This ancient cup-marked mono-lith bears a wheel disc that looks like a sun-burst. It stands outside Tain museum and may or may not have a Pictish connection. NH 780 822.

9 Nonakiln ✢ ✢ C.I. This was once sited in an ancient chapel in Roskeen parish at NH 663 712. It is now lost but a cast exists in **NMS** IB 216.
PS: a double-disc and possibly another double-disc.

10 Poolewe C.I. This was found lying in the kirkyard of Poolewe Church in 1994 by Ian Fisher, RCAHMS. NG 860 810. It was an important find which, together with the **Gairloch stone**, goes far to prove the presence of Picts in these parts after or before AD 500 when the Scots arrived from Ireland.
PS: a crescent & V-rod.

11 Roskeen (*Clach a' Mheirlich* or The Thief's Stone) C.I. Sandstone. 6 ft (183 cm) high. Prehistoric monolith used by Picts. It is sited in a field just over a mile west of Invergordon at NH 681 690.
PS: an almost unidentifiable crescent and tongs on the left side with a stepped rectangle on the front.

12 Shandwick (*Clach a' Charridh* or Stone of the Monument)
C.II. Greyish green sandstone. 9 ft (274 cm) high. 8th-century. Cross-slab encased in a glass box in a field over-looking Shandwick village. NH 856 747.

Front: a cross ornamented with spiral work contains 54 raised bosses of assorted sizes. On the left and right of the top arms the images are too worn to decipher. In the background of the shaft find two framed cherubim and a pair of interlacing serpents. Below left, a beast is trampling on a serpent (or the lion breathing life into its young). On the right, another beast may be swallowing a serpent. Below, find serpentine knotwork in very high relief. Under the cross four pairs of serpents form four large bosses, two of which to the right are completely defaced.

Back: so different in style that one wonders if the eight superb panels, five of which are visible, were carved by a different sculptor. From the top find (1) a double-disc ornamented with spirals above; (2) a Pictish beast with part of crest ornamented with keywork and two horned sheep between its legs with a third in front of its jaws; (3) a magnificent hunting scene with 8 men and 14 creatures fitted into the panel; (4) arguably the finest example of spiral decoration in Pictish art, showing 52 triple spirals arranged symmetrically in concentric circles with C- and S-shaped connections ornamented with almond-shaped and triangular spots in the spaces between the spirals; (5) interlace composed of circular knotwork; (6) key-pattern and (7) shows four serpentine creatures with beast heads interlaced to form loops and plaits while (8) has four serpents with interlaced bodies.

13 Strathpeffer Eagle Stone (*Clach 'n Tuideain* or Stone of the Turning) C.I. Contorted blue gneiss 2 ft 8 in (81 cm) high. This stands in a field east of the village centre. Well sign-posted. NH 485 585.

PS: an arch like a horseshoe above an eagle symbol.

History: Many legends. The Brahan Seer prophesied that if it fell a third time, the Strathpeffer valley would be flooded. It is now probably on its third site and firmly cemented into place.

14 Tarbat Old Church Historic Trust, Portmahomack.

Soon to be the focal point of a prestigious Heritage Centre. Ten fragments of grey-green sandstone, 8th or 9th century, have been found in and around the church. NH 915 840. The site has been associated with St Colman, from whom the village of Portmahomack (Portmacholmag) may take its name. He may have founded a monastery here bringing scribes and illuminators among his followers from Northumbria, but this is at the moment speculation awaiting further excavation.

14.1: ✣ **C.II** fragment of a cross-slab. **NMS** IB 190.
Front: part of a horse and rider above a seal-like creature above two beasts. The border is similar to a vine scrolling on Hilton of Cadboll.
Right Side: a crescent & V-rod, tuning fork or broken sword, snake & z-rod above an unrecognisable beast.

14.2-9: ✣ are all fragments of several smashed cross-slabs. **NMS**

14.10: ✣ part of a cross-slab with nine lines of letters carved in relief in Hiberno-Saxon capitals. **NMS** IB 286. The Latin inscription reads as follows:

IN NOMINE
IHESU CHRISTI
CRUX CHRISTI
IN COMMEMORATIONE
REO(TE)TII
REQUIESC (IT)

which translates roughly thus: 'In the name of Jesus Christ, the Cross of Christ, in memory of Reotetii, may he rest in peace.' Reotetii may have been the same *Reothaide Ab Ferna* whose death is recorded in 762 or 763 in the annals of Ulster and Tigernach. Usually thought to have been the Abbot of Ferns in Ireland, he may be connected to the monastery at Fearn near Edderton (which in the 13th century was removed by Farquhar, 1st Earl of Ross to a better site known as New Fearn in the Parish of Tarbat). It is a stone of the greatest importance because it shows a scriptorial connection with the illuminated Gospel manuscripts such as *Lindisfarne*. It adds strength to the conjecture that the *Book of Kells* itself may have been completed in one of the monasteries of Easter Ross before its removal to Ireland.

Some further fragments found in 1993 are now in the care of Tarbat Historical Trust in the old church.

Aumbry: within a room to the left of the church entrance find a small wall cupboard which contains a panel of delicate and delightful interlace. Don't miss it.

Comment: It is clear from the wealth of fragments that Easter Ross must have been one of the most important Christian sites in Pictland. Current excavations (1994 and 1995) west of Tarbat Kirkyard by Professor Martin Carver of York University, excavator of the Sutton Hoo ship burials, have revealed foundations of what may be part of a large Pictish settlement, but this is only the beginning of a ten-year project to find the monastic settlement. During the 1995 dig another superb ?C.III stone was discovered in the wall of the crypt. It is thought there may be many more.

15 Torgorm ✤ C.I. Sandstone. Fragment from Torgorm near Conon Bridge on the far west of the Black Isle. NH 559 549. **Inverness Museum**.
PS: two double-discs & Z-rods.

CAITHNESS
AND SUTHERLAND

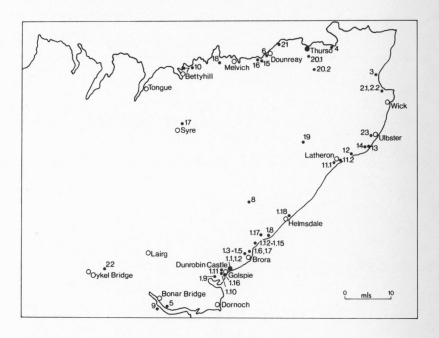

1 Dunrobin Castle Museum, Golspie, contains one of the best collections of Pictish stones in Scotland. Situated in the garden of the great castle raised by the dukes and duchesses of Sutherland, the Georgian stone museum was built as a summer house for 21-year old William, Lord Strathnaver, in 1732, and a back room added when the building was converted into a museum in 1879.

OPEN: during the summer months.

The following stones are to be seen in the Museum:

1.1: ✤ C.I. 3½ ft (107 cm) tall. It was found in 1854 by workmen near the beach west of the kitchen garden wall. It is thought to have been a capstone over a cist grave which contained the skeletons of two men. NC 849 006.
PS: a salmon, broken sword, mirror & comb.

1.2 'The Princess Stone': ✤ C.I. *c.* 4 ft (122 cm) tall. This was ploughed up in 1977 at the Dairy Park below Dunrobin Castle. Dr Close-Brooks' excavation associated the stone with a low cairn which had covered the body of a woman in a stone-lined grave. NC 849 005.
PS: a double crescent, snake & Z-rod, mirror & comb.

Clynekirkton

1.3: ✤ C.I. Red sandstone. 4¼ ft (130 cm) tall. It was found well-preserved in Clyne churchyard in 1855 at NC 894 060.
PS: a crescent & V-rod, and rectangle.

1.4: ✤ C.I. 4 ft (122 cm) tall. It was found in Clyne churchyard in 1868 but is said to have been removed there from Clynemilton Farm by a crofter. NC 894 060.
PS: a rectangle, crescent & V-rod, and mirror.

1.5: ✤ C.III. 1 ft (30 cm) tall. Purple sandstone. Fragment of a cross-slab found in 1877 and built into the east gable wall of Clyne church. NC 894 060.
Front: the head of a carved cross set within a rounded top with squared stepped hollows in the armpits. A double incised ring links the square arms. The cross is decorated with a continuous pattern of spirals.
Back: smooth and plain.

Clynemilton

1.6: ✤ C.I. Sandstone. 5½ ft (168 cm). This was found before 1860 on Clynemilton Farm at NC 914 069.
PS: an arch at top in centre, a crescent & V-rod, and mirror.

1.7: ✤ C.I. Sandstone. 3 ft (157 cm) tall. This was found before 1860 at same site as above. NC 914 069.
PS: top left, a notched rectangle & Z-rod: top right, a mirror & comb.

1.8 Collieburn: ✤ C.III. 5 ft 2 in (157 cm) high. The lower part of cross-slab, found in 1869, while excavating for the railway near Collieburn *c.* 6 miles (9.7 km) north of Brora on A9.
Front: a key-pattern above four linked circles of double-beaded knotwork. The lower part is plain except for a single incised swastika, which Romilly Allen suggests may have been a stone-maker's mark, but Norse not Pictish. The stone may have been broken to form a door jamb.
Back: as above, but without the key-pattern and swastika.

1.9 Craigton: ✤ C.I. Sandstone. 6½ ft (198 cm) tall. Found by the plough before 1834 in Craigton field *c.* NH 795 986, this stone now stands outside by a woodland path east of the castle. NH 852 008.
PS: part of a small notched rectangle, large crescent & V-rod set sideways, and a small flower with two branches.

1.10 Golspie: ✤ C.I. *c.* 4 ft (122 cm) tall. This stone was ploughed up in field (now built over) north of Golspie Main St in 1942 at NC 834 002. It was used as a capstone for a short cist. The flaking surface makes the symbols hard to see.
PS: a crescent & V-rod, Pictish beast, and mirror and comb.

1.11 Golspie: ✤ C.II. 6 ft (183 cm) tall. An intriguing cross-slab with a long history. It was drawn by the Revd Charles Cordiner in 1780 when it was lying in Golspie churchyard. NH 837 002. It was probably used as tombstone for a Robert Gordon in 1630, and was taken to Dunrobin in 1868.
Front: a Latin cross with circular hollow armpits, containing five panels of decoration. The background is divided into nine panels. Left of the shaft and above the cross, the ornamentation has been defaced to make way for a modern inscription which reads HEIR IS THE BURIAL PLEAC TO ROBERT GORDON ELDEST SON TO ALEX GORDON OF SUTHE(RLAND).

Back: from the top find a rectangle, Pictish beast, Pict man with double-headed axe and dirk confronting a lion and a fish, a flower, a small crescent & V-rod, a large double-disc and two intertwined adders biting their own fish tails.

Front frame: Ogam inscription runs up the right side and along the top which might translate as 'all holy to the memory of ?A son of ?B'.

Sides: a spiral border pattern.

Kintradwell

1.12: ✤ **C.I.** Sandstone. *c.* 3 ft (91 cm). Long-shaped fragment found in 1864 *c.* 100 yards (91 m) west of Kintradwell broch, between the railway and the sea at NC 928 081.

PS: S-shaped symbol, disc and notched rectangle.
Comment: Kintradwell is associated with the legendary St Tredwell or Triduana. She may have accompanied St Curadan-Boniface from Northumberland to King Nechtan mac Derile's court *c.* 710 and became an abbess or hermit in Perthshire and died in Restalrig (Edinburgh). Churches dedicated to her include Kintradwell and Papa Westray (Orkney). Many legends associated with her are found in the Aberdeen Breviary. (Some believe her to have been a pagan goddess.)

1.13: ✤ **C.I.** Iron-coloured sandstone. This was found in 1873 to the north-east of Kintradwell broch at NC 93 16.
PS: S-shaped symbol, part of a cauldron.

1.14: ✤ **C.I.** Red sandstone. 3½ ft (107 cm). An oval fragment found in 1872, also at NC 93 16.
PS: a crescent & V-rod, mirror with comb beneath. Dr Close-Brooks suggests the lay-out is uncommon, but part of the surface may have flaked away.

1.15: ✤ **C.I.** Fragment found in 1873 on the same site as 1.13 and 1.14.
PS: part of a broken sword or tuning fork.

Little Ferry Links

1.16: ✤ **C.I** fragments found between 1872 and 1880 on the south side of Ferry Road in Golspie.
PS: (1) part of a rectangle (2) very worn part of a crescent, terminal of a V- or Z-rod (3) a small fragment with part of a disc (4) a fine terminal of V-rod and the edge of a crescent. A fifth fragment which fits 1.16 was recognised

in **Inverness Museum** and may be seen there. Part of a crescent and small part of a disc.

1.17 Lothbeg: ✤ C.III. Purple sandstone. Triangular fragment of a small cross-slab found in 1869 while constructing a railway near Collieburn at NC 94 10.
Front: part of the left arm of a cross and ring with a key pattern.
Back: the right arm of a cross with squared stepped armpits and filled with interlace.

1.18 Navidale: ✤ C.I. Purple sandstone. It was noticed in 1968 or 1969 lying against a graveyard wall, which was once part of St Ninian's Chapel (destroyed in 1556). ND 042 162.
PS: a cauldron above a beast. Very worn.

2 Ackergill
2.1: ✤ (also known as **Keiss Bay**) C.I. This was found in 1896 in bits at Links of Keiss Bay. ND 348 550. **NMS** IB 168.
PS: the lower part of a salmon, rectangle and a line of eight Ogam letters as follows: N E H T E T R E.

2.2: ✤ Small fragments of grey slate found at ND 349 550. **NMS** IB 206.
PS: a notched rectangle.

3 Birkle Hill, Keiss. ✤ C.I. This was found in 1895 in one of two mounds of sand *c.* 8 miles (12.9 km) north of Wick at ND 339 585. **NMS** IB 188
PS: possibly a mirror ornamented with simple flower-like decoration Beside it, a triple oval with intersecting arcs of circles.

4 Craig of Hattel ✤ C.I. 6 ft (183 cm). This once stood at Castleton 5 miles (8 km) east of Thurso at ND 188 690 and bore the effigy of, possibly, a greyhound. Lost before 1873.

5 Creich EC. 8 ft (244 cm) high. Slab with an incised cross on the north side of Dornoch Firth *c.* 3 miles (4.8 km) east of Bonar Bridge. NH 637 892.

6 Dounreay ✤ Fragment of a decorated slab found west of Thurso. **NMS** IB 303.

7 Farr C.III. Blue schistose slate containing bits of quartz. 7½ ft (229 cm) high. This cross-slab stands in Farr churchyard on the north coast of Sutherland, north-east of Bettyhill at NC 714 623.

Front: a highly decorated ringed cross on a shaft with an arched base. It is divided into three panels with a key pattern. The space within the base is filled with two birds, their necks gracefully twisted together and their heads looking in different directions. Romilly Allen tells us that the bottom panel of key pattern, measuring just over a foot (30cm) square, contains no less than 655 straight lines and 496 small triangles.

Vertical side: a man on horseback, a tree with beast on each side, a sheep, a man on foot and two riders on one horse, a pair of angels.

Vertical end: indecipherable, but possibly two angels.

8 Kildonan Cross stands in the beautiful but desolate Strath of Kildonan on the A897 about 9 miles (14.5 km) north-west of Helmsdale at NC 911 209.

9 Kincardine, Ardgay. **C.III.** 5 ft (152 cm) long by *c.* 1 ft (30 cm) high and 2 ft (61 cm) wide. Very worn fragment sculptured in relief on two faces. This once stood in the kirkyard of the now disused church *c.* 1 mile (1.6 km) south-east of Bonar Bridge at NH 605 894. It is currently awaiting conservation and placement in a suitable site.

10 Kirtomy ✚ Stone on the north coast of Sutherland about a mile off the A836 between Armadale and Bettyhill at NC 74 64. It was sketched by the sister of the minister at Farr and sent to Revd Dr Joass of Golspie in 1890. It is thought to have been built into a barn at Kirtomy. It displayed a serpent. Lost.

11 Latheron
    11.1: ✚ **C.II.** Part of a cross-slab, found in an old byre at Latheron in 1903. ND 198 332. **NMS** IB 183.
Front: a cross shaft filled with interlace.
PS: an eagle, a salmon, two riders, some Ogam letters.

    11.2: C.I. This slab forms the lintel of a false window in the south gable of the farmhouse at Latheron. ND 199 334.
PS: a crescent & V-rod.

12 Lybster Church EC. This rough boulder, in a lean-to shelter beside the church, is incised with an equal-armed cross. ND 247 361 on the A9 about 5 miles (8 km) north of Latheron.

13 Mid Clyth Cemetery EC. 6 ft (183 cm). Incised cross at ND 296 372. Worn and covered with lichen.

14 Mid Clyth Greenhill Farm EC. *c.* 18 in (46 cm) long. Corner-stone on its side, about 4 ft (122 cm) up the wall of the farm out-building at ND 294 372.

15 Reay C.III. Grey sandstone. *c.* 6 ft (183 cm) tall. *c.* 10th century. Cross-slab found in Reay old burial ground, lying horizontally over an 18th-century grave. It is now sited in the west wall of old Reay chapel. NC 960 649.

16 Sandside ✢ C.I. Hard local sandstone. 4½ ft (137 cm) tall. It was found in about 1850 on the links just north of Reay. It was removed to Sandside Farm to cover the mill lade where the road crossed over it, and was later taken to Sandside House in 1889 at NC 952 652.
PS: a triple oval, disc & notched rectangle, mirror & comb.

17 Strathnaver EC. 2⅓ ft (71 cm) high. Short granite pillar with a rounded top and equal-armed incised cross. It is said to mark the grave of the 'Red Priest'. Find it 30 miles (48 km) north of Lairg on the Bettyhill Road B871 between Rhifail and Syre at NC 714 472.

18 Strathy EC. Sandstone. 4½ ft (137 cm) long. Cross with rounded ends to the shaft and arms, and a circular depression in the middle of the arms, found on the north coast of Sutherland, lying on a moor just south-west of Strathy church at NC 831 650.

19 Thulachan EC. stone broken into two pieces with the shaft of an incised cross on one piece and the top arm of a cross on the other. The three remaining arms would seem to have sunk underground. Situated 4 miles (6.5 km) out in the Flow Country behind locked forest gates at ND 105 395.
   Comment: This cross used to be a gathering place for clansmen on thieving raids, but may also have been the centre of a Christian settlement long ago deserted.

20 Thurso Museum shelters two of the finest stones in the area.

20.1 Ulbster: ✤ C.II. ORS. *c.* 5 ft (152 cm). 8th-century cross-slab, which originally stood in Ulbster kirkyard, attached to the ruined church of St Martin. ND 325 410. It was removed to an exposed mound at Thurso Castle and finally to **Thurso Museum**.

Front: a very worn equal-armed decorated cross on a shaft with a rectangular base. Background above the arms, two animals; the beast on the left is indecipherable, the one on the right looks like a cow. On each side of the lower arms two beasts face each other. Left of the shaft, two men kneel on either side of a ?chalice or possibly a hanging bowl with the snake symbol below them. Right of the shaft, a flower symbol with three shoots is set above part of a horse and ?colt with its legs doubled up beneath it. The top front has been mutilated by deeply-cut Gothic letters which spell 'Ulbster Stone'.

Back: an equal-armed decorated cross surrounded by an array of symbols, reading clockwise from top left as follows: Pictish beast above a salmon; decorated crescent & V-rod above a lion or cat-like creature in the top right; double-disc above two crescents back-to-back at the right of the lower arm of the cross; seahorse and step symbol to the left of the lower arm. In all, Ulbster displays eight symbols.

20.2 Skinnet 1: ✤ C.II. Sandstone. 7½ ft (229 cm) tall. Cross-slab which originally stood at St Thomas' Chapel, Skinnet, Halkirk ND 131 621. It was moved to **Thurso Museum** sometime after 1861, where it lay under a bookcase in six fragments piled on top of each other. Eventually it was put together to form a beautiful but worn stone.

Front: a decorated equal-armed cross on a long shaft with a square base. Between the four arms are four ornamented discs. In the background to the shaft, two seahorses face each other. Their jaws are woven into decoration on the shaft, their manes are interlaced while their tails are curled into spirals. Below the base, a very worn horse.

Back: a smaller gracefully decorated equal-armed cross on a shaft with a square base. Below the base, find a triple oval symbol and an elaborate crescent & V-rod.

21 Thurso Castle or **Crosskirk** ✣ **C.I.** Said to have been found outside the ancient church of St Mary, Lybster in Reay. ND 025 701. It is thought to have been given to the King of Denmark by Sir George Sinclair. Lost.
PS: a crescent & V-rod above an arch.

22 Tutim EC. 4 ft (122 cm) long. Recumbent gravestone with an incised armpit cross in Strath Oykel. NC 435 015.

23 Watenan ✣ **C.I.** Fragments with part of a crescent & V-rod, found at a low round cairn. ND 312 408. These were in the **John Nicolson Museum** near Aukengill at ND 368 637 in 1991, but check first with **Thurso Museum**.

ORKNEYS

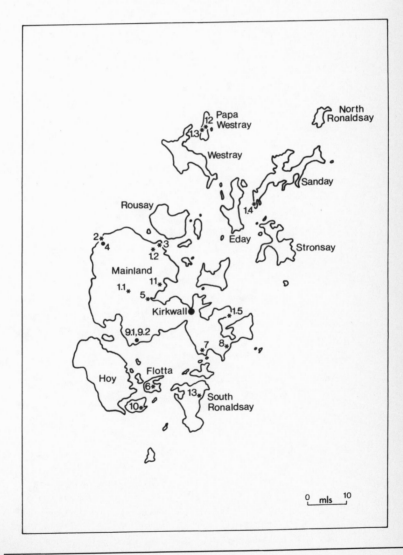

North
Ronaldsay

Papa
12 Westray
13

Westray

Sanday

1.4

Rousay

Eday

Stronsay

2
4
3
1.2

Mainland
11
1.1
5

Kirkwall
1.5

9.1, 9.2

7 8

Hoy
Flotta
6

10
13 South
Ronaldsay

0 ___ mls ___ 10

Orkneys

1 Tankerness House Museum Kirkwall displays five stones and fragments with a large number of Pictish artifacts, many from the important excavation of Buckquoy. This is one of the most enjoyable and informative museums in Scotland.

OPEN: weekdays throughout the year from 10.30 am–12.30 pm and 1.30–5 pm from May to September. The museum opens on Sundays from 2–5 pm. The following stones are to be seen there:

1.1 Knowe of Burrian: ✤ **C.I.** 3⅔ ft (112 cm) high. This was found during the excavation of a broch on Mainland, 1936. HY 308 168. Burrian also produced a small ox-bone with a crescent and V-rod on one side, and disc with notched rectangle on the other, thought to be a playing piece.
PS: an eagle, a crescent & a V-rod, and a mirror.

1.2 Evie: ✤ **C.I.** Rousay flagstone. Fragment found on the Sands of Evie at 1967. HY 372 264.
PS: pecked out mirror and three discs.

1.3 Papa Westray: ✤ **C.II.** Cross-slab found on the shore near St Boniface's Church in 1992 and thought by Dr Raymond Lamb to be part of a corner-post shrine. HY 490 530.
PS: a rectangle and part of a cross.

1.4 Pool: ✤ **C.I.** Rousay flagstone. 6th century. This was found on Sanday during the excavation of a multi-period settlement site and re-used as a paving stone inside a pre-Norse structure. HY 619 379.
PS: a double-disc and several discs.

1.5 Tankerness Ness: ✤ **C.I.** Yellow sandstone. Fragment found in a garden *c.* 1986 at the original Tankerness site. HY 545 093.
PS: a seahorse.

2 Brough of Birsay ✤ **C.II. ORS.** 6 ft (183 cm) tall. Fragments found in 1935 in St Peter's Chapel kirkyard on the small, tidal island of Birsay. Thin fragments may have broken off a thicker slab with the front bearing a cross. HY 240 285. Mended, the stone is on display in **NMS** IB 243. A cast is erected on site.
PS: a disc and rectangle, a crescent and V-rod, a Pictish

beast, an eagle. Below, three figures with spears and rectangular shields process from left to right. The leading figure is thought to represent a king. Note his artificially curled hair, elaborate shield and embroidered hemline. The middle figure is bearded, while the third man seems younger. The symbols may represent divine kingship with power over the sun, moon, water and air. The leading figure may symbolise the Pictish ideal of sovereignty – King David followed by his sons Absalom and Jonathan. Alternatively the figures may stand for one king in three stages of his life, but this can only be speculation.

3 Broch of Gurness ✤ **C.I.** Fragment found during excavation of the broch in 1935, close to the site of a cemetery. It was recognised as possibly Pictish in 1967, and is now in the **site museum** in the parish of Evie and Rendall. HY 382 269.
PS: set horizontally reading from the left; rectangle, disc & notched rectangle, rectangle containing two head-to-head skittle-like objects.

4 Broch of Oxtro ✤ slab was found covering a cist burial during excavation of the broch before 1874. It was possibly built into the wall of farm offices at Boardhouse in the parish of Birsay at HY 254 268. Lost.
PS: an eagle.

5 Burness ✤ stone was originally found near Finstown 7 miles (11.3 km) north-west of Kirkwall at HY 35 14. It displays incised markings and a small figure. **NMS** IB 201.

6 Flotta Island ✤ **C.III.** Grey sandstone. 5 ft 5 in (165 cm) long by 2 ft 8 in (81 cm) wide. Possible altar frontal found on the ?site of an ancient church at ND 36 94. **NMS** IB 48.
Front: a raised border round edge. A Celtic cross with rounded armpits in the centre. The top, bottom and right arms of the cross are decorated with interlace.

7 Graemeshall, St Marys Holm. ✤ **C.III.** 4¾ ft (145 cm) high. Cross-slab fixed to the north wall in a private chapel. Access is available. HY 487 017.
Front: an equal-armed cross with varied decoration on the right arm. The shaft and square base are set within a flat raised moulding. The other three arms are badly defaced.

8 Green's Stone ✤ C.I. Hard yellowish flagstone. 6 ft (183 cm) tall. This was found in 1923, lying face-down underground in the parish of St Andrews and Deerness at HY 542 032. **NMS** IB 203.
PS: a disc and notched rectangle, a crescent & V-rod and a mirror.

9 Orphir Stones ✤ C.I. Two stones, according to J.S. Richardson's notes in 1939, were found during excavations at Orphir at HY 334 043.

9.1: a crescent and V-rod.

9.2: 'was built into the north-west corner of the pend tower' and bore a crescent and V-rod and rectangle. Both lost.

10 Osmundwall, Isle of Hoy. ✤ **EC.** Discovered in the foundations of St Colm's Chapel, Kirkhope, Walls. **NMS** IB 169.

11 Redland, Firth ✤ C.I. Clay site. 3 ft (91 cm) high. Fragment found in 1864 built into a cottage wall just north of Finstown at HY 378 171. **NMS** IB 24.
PS: a rectangle above a crescent & V-rod.

12 St Boniface Church ✤ Incised cross from Island of Papa Westray at HY 490 530. **NMS** IB 200.

13 St Peter's Church, South Ronaldsay. ✤ **C.I.** Sandstone. 5 ft (152 cm) high. ND 471 908. This formed a window-sill in the church until 1852 when removed to **NMS** IB 2.
Front: an ornamented rectangle above a crescent and V-rod.
Back: a worn crescent & V-rod above a disc & notched rectangle.

SHETLANDS

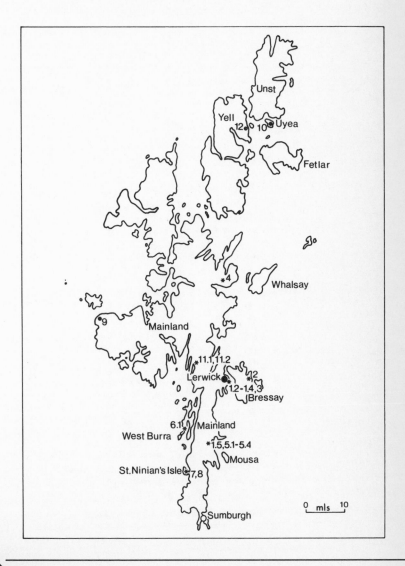

Unst

Yell
12 10 Uyea

Fetlar

Whalsay

*4

9

Mainland

*11.1,11.2

Lerwick *2
1.2-1.4,3
Bressay

6.1
West Burra *Mainland
*1.5,5.1-5.4
Mousa
St.Ninian's Isle 7,8

Sumburgh

0 mls 10

Shetlands

1 The Shetland Islands Council Museum Service takes care of three museums. The building at Lower Hillhead, Lerwick, gives an excellent introduction to the Picts in Shetland. Although most of the Shetland stones are in **NMS** Edinburgh, you will be able to see a selection of more recently discovered finds there.

OPEN: 10am – 7pm every weekday.

The following stones are in the museum:

1.2 Papil: ✢ **C.III. ORS.** 5⅓ ft (163 cm) tall. The fragment of a cross-slab found in a churchyard. The design on it is found frequently in Ireland and Iona.

. *Front:* an incised ringed cross with expanded ends to the arms and two concentric circles in the centre.

1.3 Papil or **The Monk Stone:** ✢ **C.III.** Rectangular shrine frontal in **Lerwick Museum**.

Front: Left to right, a small free-standing cross with a decorated centre on a rectangular base. The cross is approached by a procession of five cowled Columban monks, similar to those on Papil 6.1. The fourth is mounted, while the fifth bears a Bible satchel round his neck. All except the rider carry staffs – ?croziers. Below the figures are four linked pairs of spirals.

1.4 Papil: ✢ Incised cross-slab surmounted by a double scroll.

1.5 Mail Figure Stone, Cunningsburgh. ✢ ?**C.I. ORS.** This was found in August 1992 by a grave-digger in Mail Chapel graveyard at HU 433 279. It is difficult to date but possibly early 7th century. It is now in **Lerwick Museum**.

Description: a finely incised figure of a sparsely-bearded man with a wolf or dog muzzle (which may be a mask) and 15 triangular teeth. He carries an axe in his right hand and a knob-headed stick or club in his left. He wears an elaborate tunic with a decorated hem that reaches just above his knees. His legs and feet are bare.

Comment: This is possibly Shetland's most important find since the St Ninian's Isle Treasure, and it can be compared with other animal-headed figures, such as the two bird-headed men on the Papil Stone. Dr Anna Ritchie suggests that in early religions it was often the custom for the king to take over role of a god. 'Pictish sculpture suggests very strongly that animal and bird masks played a part in pagan ceremonies'. Val Turner, Shetland archaeologist, suggests that the single standing figure may be another symbol comparable to the crescent or double-disc (*See* Rhynie Man).

2 Bressay ✦ **C.III** (possibly II). Chlorite schist. 3¾ ft (114 cm) high. Cross-slab found at Cullingsburgh (Culbinsburgh) on the north-east side of Bressay Island at HU 522 424. It is thought to have been discovered by workmen near site of the ruined church of St Mary. After many removals, it was finally sent to Edinburgh in 1864. **NMS** IB 109.
Front: an equal-armed cross and spaces between filled with interlace and contained within a circle. Above, in each corner, two bug-eyed monsters are disgorging and swallowing a man who is stretched between them. Under the cross, two monks with Bible satchels and crooks face each other over a smaller mounted man. The monks have two symbols carved above their croziers – a small incised cross and an S-shaped design. Below the figures, there is a small piece of plait-work, a large lion-like figure and a small fat ?pig.
Back: three panels as follows: (1) an interlaced circular cross surrounded by a rectangular frame of double twisted loops; (2) two lion-like beasts with open jaws facing each other; (3) two monks similar to pair on front with book-satchels.
Edges: contain scholastic Ogam inscriptions.

3 Lerwick ✦ ✦ **?C.I.** Tiny fragment with incised patterns on both sides. The original site is unknown. At one time it was in Lerwick Museum then sent to **NMS** and catalogued as IB 19. There is no mention of it in the *List of Dark Age Sculpture in RMS* (1981). Probably lost.

4 Lunasting ✦ Sandstone slab found in a cottage in the north Mainland in 1867, HU 472 650. Ogam inscription. **NMS** IB 113.

5 Mail, Cunningsburgh, HU 433 279 was a very important **EC** site. Buildings and hearths together with three Ogam stones, three runic stones and one Pictish stone have been found at Chapel Mail cemetery. There could be many more. **Lerwick Museum**.

5.1: ✤ *See* **Lerwick Museum**.

5.2: ✤ ?C.I. Greyish sandstone. Fragment with three Ogam letters on one side and part of a possible rectangle symbol on the other. **NMS** IB 114.

5.3: ✤ fragment of a slab with two lines of Ogam inscription. **NMS** IB 115.

5.4: ✤ fragment with parts of three lines of Ogam inscription. **NMS** IB 182.

6 Papil in West Burra Island, some 12 miles (19 km) south-east of Scalloway, is thought to have been an important Columban monastic site. HU 36 32. The name comes from Norse word *papi,* a hermit. Four Papil stones were recovered from the kirkyard and date from the 7th (possibly) to 10th centuries. 1.2, 1.3 and 1.4 are seen in **Lerwick Museum**.

6.1: ✤ C.III. Reddish sandstone. 6 ft 10 in (208 cm) high. A cross-slab found in 1877 at HU *c.* 36 32. Now in **NMS** IB 46.

Front: three panels; (1) a wheel-headed cross with expanded arms set within a circle except at the bottom where it joins a short shaft. The cross is undecorated, but almond-shaped spaces between its arms are filled with interlace. The bottom of the shaft contains a piece of knotwork resembling an elaborate figure-of-eight. Shaft background – two pairs of Columban monks with pointed cowls and crooks. Outer figures shoulder book-satchels; (2) a beast with spiralled joints, a protruding tongue and a tail curled over its back. Possibly lion symbol of St Mark as illustrated in the *Book of Durrow,* Folio 191v; (3) two creatures with human bodies, arms, axes and heads, but with bird beaks and legs. The beaks (or bird-masks) support or peck the ears of a human head. They were perhaps intended to be demons, whispering evil thoughts into Christian ears.

7 St Ninians Isle Treasure ✤ This beautiful island, which should not be missed, is reached by a tombola of fine white sand. The small ruined church dates from *c.* 11th century, but there was an earlier building below it. A hoard of 27 exquisite Pictish silver objects was found in 1958. These were acquired (after opposition) by **NMS**.

8 St Ninian's Isle Stone ✢ A sandstone slab with Ogams, found in burial ground near the site of St Ninian's chapel in 1876. HU 368 208. **RMS** IB 112.

9 Sandness ✢ C.I. This was noticed in the wall of Sandness Church near the west point of the mainland, some 20 miles (32 km) north-west of Lerwick at HU 19 57. It was mentioned in the Revd George Low's *Tour through the Islands of Orkney and Shetland* 1774. Lost.
PS: a rectangle, arch and mirror.

10 Uyea ✢ ?C.III. Dark steatite. 4 in (10 cm) long. This was found on the small island of Uyea off the south point of Unst, and sent to **NMS** in 1868, where it was catalogued under IB 18, but not mentioned in the 1981 list. It is thought to have been part of a larger stone which may have covered an urn containing burnt bones. Lost.
　　Front: the centre of a triple spiral.
　　Back: three spirals and lattice-work patterns forming lozenges and triangles.

11 Whiteness
　　11.1: ✢ Part of cross slab found *c.* 10 miles (16 km) north of Lerwick on the A971 at HU 40 46. **NMS** IB 248.

　　11.2: ✢ Fragment of slab with relief sculpture and Ogam inscription. **NMS** IB 256.

12 Yell ✢ Stone found *c.* 1850 at south Garth on the east side of the north of Yell. It was described in a lecture given by Thomas Irvine of Midbrake in 1859 as a 'very curious and remarkable stone found. . . by a tenant digging peats. It was a thin slab between 3 (91 cm) and 4 ft (122 cm) long. . . Both sides were completely covered with figures in relief having a border all round carved in zig-zag diamond and spiral lines.' By 1863 it was lost.

THE WESTERN ISLES

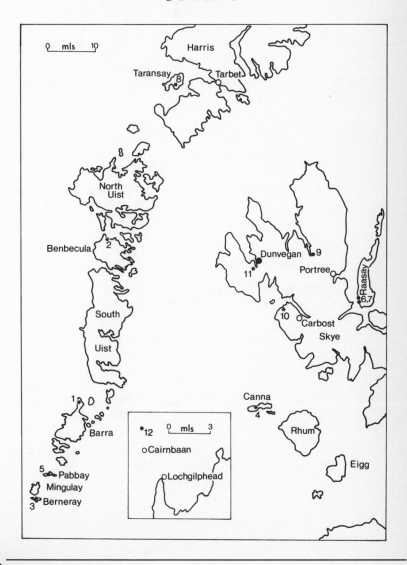

Barra

1 Kilbar, Isle of Barra. ✢ **C.III.** Greenish slate. 4½ ft (137 cm) tall. Cross-slab found in ancient burial ground in 1865 at the north end of the island. NF *c.* 705 073. **NMS** IB 102.
Front: a cross decorated in four-cord plait-work with small round hollows in armpits. Shaft background; spiral-work which develops into key-pattern.
Back: runic inscription placed vertically translates *Ur and Thur set up (these) stones of Kiskurs. May Christ (guard his soul).*

Benbecula (Strome Shunnamal)

2 Strome Shunnamal, Benbecula. ✢ **C.I** Granite. 3 ft (91 cm) long by 2½ ft (76 cm) wide. Found on the shore near a ruined ancient building on the north-east side of the island. NF *c.* 803 566. **NMS** IB 37.
PS: a circular disc enclosing three small linked discs and a rectangle.

Berneray

3 Island of Berneray ✢ **C.III.** Blue-green gneiss. 3⅔ ft (111 cm) tall. Fragment of a cross-slab found in the churchyard of St Asaph or Kilaisen. NF 930 820. **NMS** IB 3l.
Front: a panel of plait-work above a panel of key-work.

Canna

Canna Island, south-west of Skye at NG 269 055. Of the many fragments found here probably all are Scottish rather than Pictish. One worth mentioning is a curious stone found in two pieces in the ancient burial ground of St Columba's Church in the centre of the island.

4 Serpent Stone Lower fragment of a cross-shaft shows a pair of legs interwound with a serpent up to the hem of the man's tunic. The serpent's tail ends in a spiral and its beak points upwards beneath the tunic. Above the tunic find part of triquetra.

The upper panel, found much later in 1930s, shows the top half of a man. Both pieces may be seen outside Canna House.

Pabbay

5 Pabbay Island C.I. Dioritic stone. 3 ft (91 cm) high. This lies in the graveyard of Pabbay Island (south of Barra). It was noticed by Father Allan Macdonald before 1889 after

it had been uncovered in sandstorm. NL 607 875.
PS: an incised cross with expanded side arms touching a crescent & V-rod with flower below.

Raasay
6 Raasay Island C.II. Grey granite. Cross-slab found when the road from the pier to Raasay House was first constructed. Since then a new pier has been built. The stone now stands in a rockery at Raasay House. NG 547 368.
PS: a cross set in a square with a crescent & V-rod below.

7 Raasay Old Pier. An identical cross was found incised on a rock face at the old pier below Raasay House.

Taransay
8 St Taran's Cross, Paible, Isle of Taransay, Harris. ✤ **EC.** stone with an incised cross. NG 02 01. **NMS** IB 49.

Skye
9 Clach Ard, Tote, Skye. **C.I.** This was found in use as a doorway from 1880 and recognised in 1928. It is now enclosed within protective railings at NG 421 491.
PS: a crescent & V-rod, double-disc & Z-rod, mirror & comb.

10 Fiscavaig ✤ **C.I.** Mica schist. Found on the beach at Fiscavaig on Loch Bracadale at NG 33 34. This stone belongs to **NMS** IB 213, but is currently on loan to **St Mungo's Museum of Religious Life and Art in Glasgow**.
PS: a double-disc & Z-rod, crescent & V-rod.

11 Tobar na Maor Skye. ✤ **C.I.** This partly covered a well of that name beside Dun Osdale at NG 241 465 until 1910. It is now in **Dunvegan Castle Museum**.
PS: a crescent & V-rod and two concentric circles.

Argyll
12 Dunadd, Argyll. NR 837 936. This may have been a major stronghold of the Dalriadic Scots. On a rocky outcrop which dominates access to Knapdale and Kintyre. It is thought also to have been the coronation site for Scottish kings. It shows an incised boar, a stone footprint and a rock basin.

Scotland's Regions

SHETLAND
ISLANDS

ORKNEY
ISLANDS

CAITHNESS

SUTHERLAND

WESTERN
ISLES

NAIRN

ROSS &
CROMARTY

MORAY

BANFF

BADENOCH

INVERNESS

ABERDEEN

KINCARDINE

ANGUS

PERTH

ARGYLL

FIFE

KINROSS

STIRLING

CONCLUSION

Distribution of stones

There are about 630 stones and fragments mentioned in this Guide, including those recorded as lost. I cannot claim that these are all that may exist. I have not attempted to record all the EC incised grave markers or simple crosses, and my count of all the small Elgin fragments of crosses is only a guesstimate. One or two stones turn up every year, and there are probably many more yet to be uncovered. Those that have been traced divide between the areas of Pictland as follows:

Region	C.I	C.II	C.III	EC	Others
Edinburgh (& S)	3	–	–	–	–
Fife, Kinross & Stirlingshire	9	3	31	2	24+
Around Perthshire	7	17	62	10	8
The Angus Area	11	26	56	5	21
Deeside & Stonehaven	11	4	3	0	1
Aberdeen & Grampians	46	3	0	0	1
Moray & Banff	30	2	24	?	c.50
Inverness, Nairn, Badenoch, Strathspey	22	1	3	?2	0
E & W Rossshire	7	8	29	5	?
Caithness & Sutherland	23	4	9	1	1
Orkney Area	12	2	3	2	0
Shetland Area	1	1	8	0	7
Western Isles	4	1	3	0	2
Totals	**186**	**72**	**231**	**27**	**115**

Out of the above, well over half are to be found in museums, NMS or local, while some 100 are in churches, cathedrals or churchyards. Over 40 are still on private property and permission must always be sought to see them. At least 50 have been lost while some 70 remain to be seen on outdoor sites.

Although C.I stones continued to be carved after the Christian era in the early 8th century, their distribution gives a rough guide to where the Picts were from *c.* AD 500-700. In fact, the three classes could be said to represent movements in population and other changes due to shifts in the balance of power and the coming of Christianity.

C.I stones are to be found all over Pictland but by far the greater proportion are in the Grampians and Morayshire, with a generous sprinkling on the coasts of Caithness and Sutherland and 12 in Orkney.

The majority of C.II stones are in Angus and Perthshire with only 3 in the Aberdeen area compared with 46 in C.I group. The Moray Firth area is represented by an important cluster of arguably the finest cross-slabs in Pictland with a few in Caithness and Sutherland and the Northern Isles. Their presence here and elsewhere indicate important Christian Monastic sites.

C.III stones follow much the same pattern as C.II, with the greater proportion in Perth, Angus and Fife with Moray and Ross supplying a good number in the north.

Combinations of symbols

A number of stones have only one symbol on them but this may be due to the loss of a second symbol by weathering or fragmentation. The majority of stones, however, have two symbols carved or incised on them. Many have three symbols. Most, but not all of these, include a pair of symbols with the addition of a mirror or mirror & comb, usually placed below the other two. Five stones have four symbols, one stone has five symbols. Two stones have six symbols and three stones have eight symbols on them.

Distribution of symbols

Although many have tried to find a link between certain symbols and particular districts, the distribution remains fairly even and, in my opinion, no firm conclusions can be drawn. If, for example, the 'rectangle' appears more often on stones from the Northern Isles and north of Inverness (6) with 3 in Aberdeen, this may only mean that stones bearing the symbol further south have been lost, broken or are yet to be uncovered. It does appear in the East Wemyss caves in Fife and possibly on Kirriemuir 23.1 in Angus.

A last thought

Until we know for certain what the symbols mean and why they occur on stones and what the stones represent, it is impossible to draw any firm conclusions. The field, in my opinion, is still wide open for interpretation and no theory so far propounded is necessarily the right one. Those of you who discover for yourselves the stones described in this Guide are fully entitled to come to your own conclusions. Your thoughts and ideas are as valid as the next person's. You indeed may be the one to crack the symbol code.

Good Luck!

FURTHER READING

Early Christian Monuments of Scotland J. Romilly Allen & J. Anderson. Rhind Lectures 1903. Reprinted by Pinkfoot Press, Angus 1993.

Kings and Kingship in Early Scotland M.O. Anderson. Scottish Academic Press, Edinburgh 1973.

Dark Age Sculpture J. Close-Brooks & R.B.K. Stevenson. NMS, Edinburgh 1982.

Pictish Stones in Dunrobin Castle Museum J. Close-Brooks. Available on site. Pilgrim Press, Derby 1989.

The Picts Isabel Henderson. Thames & Hudson 1967.

The Art & Function of Rosemarkie's Pictish Monuments Isabel Henderson. Groam House, Rosemarkie. 1991.

Early Christianity in Pictland Kathleen Hughes. Jarrow Lecture 1970.

The Symbol Stones of Scotland Anthony Jackson. Orkney Press 1984.

The Picts and the Scots Lloyd and Jenny Laing. Alan Sutton Publishing 1993.

Foul Hordes: The Picts in the North East Ian Ralston & Jim Inglis. University of Aberdeen 1984.

Picts Anna Ritchie. HMSO. Edinburgh 1989.

Pictish Symbol Stones A Handlist. RCAHMS 1994.

The Picts: A New Look at Old Problem. ed. Alan Small. Dundee 1987.

Warlords and Holy Men Alfred P. Smyth. Edinburgh University Press 1984 and 1989.

In Search of the Picts Elizabeth Sutherland. Illustrated by T.E. Gray. Constable Publishing 1994.

The Problem of the Picts ed. F.T. Wainwright. Nelson 1955.